KS3
English
Practice Test Papers
Ages 11-14

B C
E F
H I

Nicolas Barber

Contents

Sets
ABC

KEY STAGE 3
Levels 4–7

Introduction

English

Introduction

Introduction

Instructions on using the Practice Test Papers

Understanding Assessment

At the end of Key Stage 3 (usually in Year 9 at the age of 14), teacher assessment is used to determine your level of attainment in subjects including English, Maths and Science. There are no national tests but assessments by your teacher will help them to determine your level of attainment (see page 9).

About these Practice Test Papers

This book contains three sets of practice test papers, which provide a means of parental or self-assessment that can be easily carried out at home. The papers will help you to evaluate an approximate level of attainment, highlight opportunities for further study and skills practice that will aid improvement, and record results to track progress. The instructions and guidelines in this Introduction provide guidance on how to use the papers for self-assessment.

The questions have been written by experienced teachers and are based on the programme of study for Key Stage 3.

Sets A, B and C each provide one complete assessment. Each set comprises of:
• 1 Reading Test Paper (1 hour 15 minutes), including Reading Material
• 1 Writing Test Paper (1 hour 15 minutes), including a Short and a Long Writing Task
• 2 Shakespeare Test Papers (45 minutes)*

* This book provides papers on *Much Ado About Nothing* and *Romeo and Juliet*. Only complete the Shakespeare Test Paper that is relevant to the play you are studying.

The tests can be taken at different times, but try to complete a set all within the same week. Take the tests at a time when you can work uninterrupted and do not feel too tired.

You should complete Sets A, B and C at intervals throughout Key Stage 3. Make sure you leave a reasonable amount of time between each assessment – it is unrealistic to expect to see an improvement in just a few weeks. You will feel much more motivated if you wait for a while, because your progress will be more obvious.

If you want to re-use the practice test papers, you can write in pencil and then rub out your answers. However, do not repeat the same test paper too soon, otherwise you will remember the questions and your results will not be an accurate reflection of your abilities.

Before you start:
- find a suitable place to complete the tests – somewhere quiet, where you won't be disturbed
- make sure you have a pen, pencil, ruler, rubber and a clock or watch to time yourself
- turn off your mobile phone
- read the instructions below and those on the front of the test paper carefully.

When completing the test papers:
- try to answer all of the questions and make sure you read them carefully
- write your answers for the Reading Test in the spaces provided on the test paper
- write your answers for the Writing Test and Shakespeare Test on lined paper
- keep an eye on the time – if you spend longer than the allocated time on the paper your results will not accurately reflect your abilities.

When you have finished:
- use the answers and marks provided in the pull-out Answers and Mark Scheme to mark the test paper
- read the top tips on how to improve your performance and remember the key points
- add up the total number of marks.

These tests are similar to tests you may have taken throughout Key Stages 2 and 3.

You should check how much time you have to complete each individual test. You should choose a period when you are not too tired and can work uninterrupted. You do not have to take the tests in one sitting. The questions have been written by experienced teachers, so important ideas are revisited.

Answers should be written on the test papers in the indicated spaces. At the end of the test, the paper can be marked by referring to the Answers and Mark Scheme. When you have taken the tests, they will be helpful to use to revise and prepare for actual assessments.

Tips for the Top

Make sure you have a suitable place to do the test and have a pen, pencil and rubber.

The number of marks is shown for each part of the question.

Remember to read the questions carefully.

Short Answer Questions

These questions test a range of different skills. You will do well on this test paper by thinking about a number of things:

1   Organise your time. People who do well on this paper make sure that they spend an appropriate amount of time on each question. There are 32 marks for this paper, and you have one hour to write your answers, so you should be spending just under 2 minutes on each mark. Stick to this. If you get stuck, move on and come back to the missed questions at the end, if you have time.

2   Know what the questions require. The questions are testing different reading skills. Some require short answers, others need examples and some require a mixture. Obviously, the number of marks available and the amount of space for the answer gives some idea of how much to write, but you should also know what the different instruction words in the questions mean. Here is a range of commonly used instruction words used in this paper and what they require from you:
"Give reasons" – explain – put things in your own words.
"What does ... suggest?" – give your own personal opinion based on the way the word is used in the text.
"Explain" – what it says! Use your own words.
"Identify" – give an example, or a quotation.
"What is the effect of ...?" – give your own personal opinion based on the way the word is used in the text.
"Why is ...?" – explain – put things in your own words.

3   When filling in charts and boxes, don't put more answers than you are allowed. You will simply be given zero!

4   On the questions worth 5 marks, make sure you have a quotation and a comment on every bullet point. To get the top marks on the 5-mark questions, pick out individual words from your quotations and use those individual words to show exactly where you have got your ideas from.

The Writing Tasks

In school, all through Key Stage 3, you will have learned about different styles of writing. The long and short writing tasks are testing to see if you know how to write in different styles. This means the following:

1   Revise what you have learned in school about how to write in different styles, e.g. How do you write to:
    *   imagine, explore, entertain?
    *   argue, persuade, advise?
    *   inform, explain, describe?
    *   analyse, review, comment?

If you revise what you have done on each of these writing types, then it will help you to get more marks for "Communication and effect" which carries the most marks on both the long and short tasks.

2   Plan your answer! If you want to get good marks for paragraphing and organisation, then it is essential to do a short plan first. It doesn't matter how you plan – you could brainstorm, mind map – do whatever suits your learning style. At the very least, decide what will happen in the beginning, middle and end of your writing. If you have time, decide what you are going to put in each paragraph.

3	Leave a short amount of time to proof-read what you have written. On the short task, make sure you check spelling, because you gain marks for "Spelling" on that task.

4	You don't have to worry about writing vast amounts, especially on the short answer task. The marker is looking for quality, not quantity.

The Shakespeare Papers

Before you do a paper:
*	make sure that you understand what is happening in your scenes first
*	make sure that you know what the important quotations are in your scenes – what they are, what they mean and how you might explain them
*	know how your scenes relate to the rest of the play.

In a Shakespeare – or other Literature – exam you should do the following:

1	Read the question carefully.

2	Write on the question paper or provided text, if there is one – underline the key words in the question, or in the text. Use these to identify what you have to include in your answer. A highlighter pen would be handy!

3	Use the words you have underlined in the question to help identify the quotations you are going to use from the extracts.

4	Plan your answer – make sure you cover all parts of the question required.

5	Use a quotation for every point you make. Pick words out of the quotations where possible, because you will show more exactly where you have got your ideas from, which is essential to achieve Level 6 and Level 7.

6	To show your personal opinion on the language of the play, pick out words and use sentences like "the word … suggests to me … because …" and "the words … imply that … because …".

Frame your comments using sentence frames like these and you will be showing personal opinion and developing your ideas in depth, which should mean that you are commenting at least at Level 5 or above, depending on how thoroughly and sensibly you phrase your comments.

Using your Marks to Assess Levels

Record your test marks in the progress grid below:

	Set A Week beginning: __/__/__	Set B Week beginning: __/__/__	Set C Week beginning: __/__/__
Reading Test			
Shakespeare Test			
Reading Total			
Reading Level			
Writing Test – Short Task			
Writing Test – Long Task			
Writing Total			
Writing Level			

When you have completed all three tests in a set:
- add the marks for the Reading Test and Shakespeare Test together to give a total mark out of 50 for Reading
- add the marks for the Writing Test Short Task and Long Task together to give a total mark out of 50 for Writing.

The table below will give you an indication of your Reading, Writing and Overall levels based on your marks:

Level	Reading mark range	Writing mark range	Overall
No level	0–7	0–4	0–10
3	8–10	5–10	11–15
4	11–16	11–12	16–30
5	17–26	13–22	31–50
6	27–33	23–31	51–65
7	34–50	32–50	66–100

Remember that the level obtained in these tests may be different from the level that your teacher reports you are working at. This is because they can only test a limited range of skills and knowledge. Your teacher will have a better idea of your overall performance. However, these tests will help you to identify areas of weakness that you can improve upon with a bit of hard work and extra study, which will help you to get a better mark on your next assessment test and progress at school.

Improving your Results and Making Progress

Go back through your test papers and make a note of all the questions that you got wrong. This will help you to identify skills that require further practice.

If you want to improve your understanding and make progress, you need to be proactive! Use Study Guides and Workbooks for home study – they include lots of practice questions, which test your knowledge, reinforce what you have learned and help to develop essential skills.

With a little bit of time and effort, when you take the next set of tests in the pack you will achieve a higher mark. Remember to record the date alongside your marks in the grid above. This will allow you to track your progress over time and will help to build your confidence and a sense of achievement.

What do Levels Mean?

Attainment levels are used to measure your progress through Key Stages 1, 2 and 3. They are concerned with your knowledge, skills and understanding of a subject.

There are eight levels and they each have a description, which sets out the skills, knowledge and understanding that you are expected to demonstrate at that level. The descriptions for Levels 1 to 8 get increasingly difficult.

Although there are eight levels, at Key Stage 3 you are generally expected to work between Levels 3 and 7, where Level 7 represents excellent knowledge, skills and understanding.

The table below shows the expected National Curriculum levels for 14 year olds.

Level	Aged 14
Level 1	
Level 2 Level 2c Level 2b Level 2a	
Level 3	Below average
Level 4	Below average
Level 5	At level expected
Level 6	At level expected
Level 7	Excellent
Level 8	Exceptional

As you can see, it is expected that a majority of 14 year olds will achieve Level 5 or 6 by the end of Year 9. If you achieve Level 7, it is a real success. A 14 year old who achieves Level 8 is working at an exceptionally high level. For comparison, a student who gains a GCSE grade C has achieved Level 7.

Your teacher will carry out regular assessments to ensure that you are working at an appropriate level and progressing at the expected rate. The test papers in this book support this process. Provided you follow the instructions and address any potential problems that the tests highlight, they will help to ensure you are always working to the best of your abilities.

Set
A

KEY STAGE 3
Levels 4–7

Reading Test
Paper

English

Food!

Reading Test Paper

Food!

Instructions:

- find a quiet place where you can sit down and complete the test paper undisturbed

- make sure you have all the necessary equipment to complete the test paper

- read the questions carefully

- answer all the questions

- go through and check your answers when you have finished the test paper

Time:

This test paper is **1 hour 15 minutes** long.

You have **15 minutes** to read the Reading Material. During this time you are not allowed to refer to the Reading Paper to look at the questions.

You have **1 hour** to write the answers.

Write the answers in this paper, then check how you have done using pages 105–107 of the Answers and Mark Scheme.

Page	19	21	23	Max. Mark	**Actual Mark**
Score	....	....	....	32	....

First name _____

Last name _____

Food!

Contents

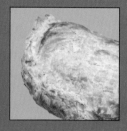

'Real' Cornish Pasties

1 The European Commission has cracked down on companies based outside Cornwall producing and selling 'Cornish' pasties. It comes after years of campaigning by the CPA (Cornish Pasty Association).

2 The name 'Cornish pasty' has now been given a PGI (protected geographical indication) status by the EC. But some producers outside Cornwall objected to the move 'cos it might have a bad effect on their sales.

3 The PGI status means that, to be called a 'Cornish pasty' the pasty has to be prepared in Cornwall. If it isn't, it can't go by the name 'Cornish pasty'!

4 A real Cornish pasty must include beef, potato, swede (also called turnip) and onion, and a pinch of salt and pepper, whilst the filling should have a thick, chunky texture.

5 Cornish pasties should be folded into a semi-circle and sealed on one side. When baked, the pastry should look tasty and golden.

6 There's no hard and fast rule on what kind of pastry should be used but a short crust pastry is often used.

7 'Cornish pasties aren't just food – they're a way of life here in Cornwall,' says top chef Meredith Gordon.

8 Cornish pasties are also known as 'oggies', 'oggins', 'teddies' and 'tiddies'.

Made in Cornwall?

9 The Cornish pasty originated in the United Kingdom, but there's some debate over whether it originally came from Cornwall or Devon.

10 The Cornish pasty is considered the national dish of Cornwall and in 2008 87 million Cornish pasties were sold by members of the CPA.

Oliver Twist

Oliver Twist is a young boy who is living in a kind of Victorian orphanage. The boys there are very badly treated and underfed. On this day, the boys decide that they want to be fed better …

1 Oliver Twist and his companions suffered the tortures of slow starvation for three months: at last they got so voracious and wild with hunger, that one boy, who was tall for his age, and hadn't been used to that sort of thing (for his father had kept a small cookshop), hinted darkly to his companions, that unless he had another basin of gruel, he was afraid he might some night happen to eat the boy who slept next him, who happened to be a weakly youth of tender age. He had a wild, hungry eye; and they implicitly believed him. A council was held; lots were cast who should walk up to the master after supper that evening, and ask for more; and it fell to Oliver Twist.

2 The evening arrived; the boys took their places. The master, in his cook's uniform, stationed himself at the copper; his pauper assistants ranged themselves behind him; the gruel was served out; and a long grace was said over the short commons. The gruel disappeared; the boys whispered to each other, and winked at Oliver; while his next neighbours nudged him. Child as he was, he was desperate with hunger, and reckless with misery. He rose from the table; and advancing to the master, basin and spoon in hand, said, somewhat alarmed at his own temerity:

3 "Please, sir, I want some more."

4   The master was a fat, healthy man; but he turned very pale. He gazed in stupefied astonishment on the small rebel for some seconds, and then clung for support to the copper. The assistants were paralysed with wonder; the boys with fear.

5   "What!" said the master at length, in a faint voice.

     "Please, sir," replied Oliver, "I want some more."

6   The master aimed a blow at Oliver's head with the ladle; pinioned him in his arms; and shrieked aloud for the beadle.

7   The board were sitting in solemn conclave, when Mr. Bumble rushed into the room in great excitement, and addressing the gentleman in the high chair, said,

8   "Mr. Limbkins, I beg your pardon, sir! Oliver Twist has asked for more!"

9   There was a general start. Horror was depicted on every countenance.

10   "For more!" said Mr. Limbkins. "Compose yourself, Bumble, and answer me distinctly. Do I understand that he asked for more, after he had eaten the supper allotted by the dietary?"

11   "He did, sir," replied Bumble.

12   "That boy will be hung," said the gentleman in the white waistcoat. "I know that boy will be hung."

From *Oliver Twist* by Charles Dickens

Why is water good for you?

The importance of drinking plenty of water and advice for adults on how much they should drink on a daily basis.

1 Water is vital for ensuring that our bodies function correctly. This is because water is responsible for transporting nutrients around the body and most of the chemical reactions within our cells take place in water.

2 As your body works it produces waste products. Some of these waste products are toxic and the body gets rid of them through the kidneys in urine, which mainly consists of water.

3 We also lose water by evaporation when we breathe and sweat. As the temperature rises and we do more activity, the amount of water lost by the body increases. To stay healthy, we must replace the fluids that we lose.

4 In moderate climates, such as the UK, we should drink at least 6 to 8 cups or glasses of water (or other fluid) to prevent dehydration. In hotter climates, your body will need more fluids to avoid becoming dehydrated.

5 Drinks that contain caffeine (such as tea, coffee and cola) can act as diuretics, which means they can make your body lose greater volumes of water than normal. As a result, these drinks can result in an increased need for water or other fluids that don't have a diuretic effect.

6 Drinks containing sugar, such as fruit juice and fizzy drinks, should also be drunk in moderation, because they can contribute to tooth decay. But, one glass of fruit juice can count towards the five portions of fruit and vegetables that we should eat each day.

1   From the first three paragraphs, give two examples of what the European Commission has done.

(2 marks)

i   _____

ii _____

2   a) In paragraph one, what does the choice of words in the following phrase suggest?
     *"The European Commission has cracked down on companies based outside Cornwall
     producing and selling 'Cornish' pasties."*   *(1 mark)*

     "crack down" suggests _____

     _____

     b) What do the words *"'cos"*, *"isn't"* and *"tasty"* suggest about the writer's audience?

     (1 mark)

     _____

     _____

3   a) The article is split into paragraphs with different topics. Complete this table by writing the
     correct paragraph number in the box next to the paragraph's topic.   *(2 marks)*

Topic	Paragraph Number
Rules about pasty ingredients	
What PGI stands for	
A reaction from a top chef	
An introduction to the article	

     b) Explain one reason why the text has paragraphs with personal comments as well as
     paragraphs about historical background.   *(1 mark)*

     _____

     _____

     _____

4   How does the article try to appeal to young people?
     You should comment on the effect of:

   - the language used

   - the length of paragraphs

   - the content of the article.   *(5 marks)*

subtotal

5 a) From the first part of the first sentence, *"Oliver Twist and his companions suffered the tortures of slow starvation for three months"*, write down one word which suggests that the boys are suffering.   *(1 mark)*

_____

   b) What is the effect of this word?   *(1 mark)*

_____

_____

_____

_____

6   In the second sentence, it says *"He had a wild, hungry eye"*. What does the phrase "hungry eye" suggest about the boy's character?   *(1 mark)*

_____

_____

_____

7 a) From the whole text, identify one feature of Oliver Twist's character.   *(1 mark)*

_____

_____

_____

   b) From the whole text, identify one feature of the master's character.   *(1 mark)*

_____

_____

_____

8 a) The extract from the story begins with long paragraphs and ends with short paragraphs.
       Explain one reason why this is.   *(1 mark)*

_____

_____

_____

_____

_____

_____

   b) Explain how the line ' *"Please, sir," replied Oliver, "I want some more"* ' makes you feel sorry
       for Oliver.   *(1 mark)*

_____

_____

_____

_____

_____

_____

_____

9   What do you learn about the writer's viewpoint and purpose from the passage? Show whether
       the following statements are TRUE or FALSE by writing T for TRUE or F for FALSE in each of
       the boxes.   *(2 marks)*

The writer wants us to feel sorry for Oliver.   ☐

The writer is trying to criticise the way that boys like Oliver
were treated by authority.   ☐

The writer is trying to give a factual historical account.   ☐

The writer is trying to entertain the reader.   ☐

10   Explain two ways that the first paragraph gives us information. Support each explanation
with a quotation.   *(2 marks)*

i   _____

_____

_____

ii   _____

_____

_____

11   How does the writer, in paragraphs three and four, try to convince the reader that drinking
water is important? Choose two different words or phrases and explain how they create this
effect on the reader.   *(2 marks)*

Word/Phrase	Effect on the reader	How it creates this effect on the reader
	makes the reader think that drinking water is important	because it suggests
	makes the reader think that drinking water is important	because it suggests

12 a) In paragraph five, what is described as the main effect of caffeine?   *(1 mark)*

_____

_____

_____

b) Why are brackets used at the start of paragraph five in the phrase *"Drinks that contain caffeine
(such as tea, coffee and cola)"*?   *(1 mark)*

_____

_____

_____

13   In this article, how are language, grammar and content used to influence the reader?
      You should comment in your answer on the effect of the following.

      • The use of scientific words and phrases.

      • Sentence lengths.

      • The use of facts.   *(5 marks)*

Q13

_____

_____

_____

_____

_____

_____

_____

_____

_____

_____

_____

_____

_____

_____

_____

_____

_____

_____

END OF TEST

subtotal

Set
A

KEY STAGE 3
Levels 4–7

Writing Test
Paper

English

Food!

Writing Test Paper

Food!

Instructions:

- find a quiet place where you can sit down and complete the test paper undisturbed
- make sure you have all the necessary equipment to complete the test paper
- read the questions carefully
- answer the questions on lined paper
- go through and check your answers when you have finished writing

Time:

This test paper is **1 hour 15 minutes** long.

You should spend **30 minutes** on the short writing task, including planning time.

You should spend **45 minutes** on the long writing task, including planning time.

Write the answers on lined paper, then check how you have done using pages 114–118 of the Answers and Mark Scheme.

Short Writing Task

Strand	Max. Mark	**Actual Mark**
Sentence structure, punctuation and text organisation	6	
Composition and effect	10	
Spelling	4	

Long Writing Task

Strand	Max. Mark	**Actual Mark**
Sentence structure and punctuation	8	
Text structure and organisation	8	
Composition and effect	14	

First name ....

Last name ....

Writing Paper – Short Writing Task

Spend about 30 minutes on this section.

You write reviews for a school magazine – this week you have been asked to write a review of one of last week's school dinners.

Here is last week's menu:

Day	Main Course	Dessert
Monday	Fish and Chips	Ice-Cream
Tuesday	Cabbage Pie & Mashed Potatoes	Grapefruit Surprise
Wednesday	Broccoli & Cucumber Salad	Rhubarb Crumble
Thursday	Pizza	Melon Juice
Friday	Chicken Curry	Chocolate Sticky Pudding

In your review, the school magazine editor wants you to:

- analyse what was in the meal

- comment on what you thought about it.

Write your review on one of the school dinners above.

(20 marks, including 4 for spelling)

Writing Paper – Long Writing Task

Spend about 15 minutes planning your answer and 30 minutes writing.

Your local area has been named the least healthy in the whole country. You are a local newspaper journalist and you have been given the job of writing an article telling people about this and persuading them to adopt a more healthy lifestyle. Here are some of the facts that you have been given:

75% of the people in your area do not take regular exercise.

85% of the people in your area eat junk food, on average, four times a week.

60% of the people in your area visit the doctor once a month.

The average life expectancy for men and women is five years below the national average.

Your editor wants you to write an article to:

• advise people about the situation in your area

• persuade them to change their ways.

Write the article.

(30 marks)

END OF TEST

Set

A

KEY STAGE 3
Levels 4–7

Shakespeare
Test Paper

English

Shakespeare Test Paper

Much Ado About Nothing

Instructions:

- find a quiet place where you can sit down and complete the test paper undisturbed

- make sure you have all the necessary equipment to complete the test paper

- read the question carefully

- answer the question on lined paper

- go through and check your answer when you have finished writing

Time:

This test paper is **45 minutes** long.

Check how you have done using pages 119–120 of the Answers and Mark Scheme.

	Max. Mark	**Actual Mark**
Score	18	....

First name ....

Last name ....

Much Ado About Nothing

You should spend about 45 minutes on this section.

Much Ado About Nothing

In these scenes, the audience see Benedick and Beatrice's relationship.

What do we learn about Benedick and Beatrice in these two scenes?

Support your ideas by referring to both of the extracts which are printed on the following pages.

(18 marks)

Use the printed scenes to answer the question set on page 29.

Act 4 Scene 1

BENEDICK	Come, bid me do anything for thee.
BEATRICE	Kill Claudio.
BENEDICK	Ha! Not for the wide world.
BEATRICE	You kill me to deny it. Farewell.
BENEDICK	Tarry, sweet Beatrice.
BEATRICE	I am gone though I am here. There is no love in you. Nay, I pray you, let me go.
BENEDICK	Beatrice –
BEATRICE	In faith, I will go.
BENEDICK	We'll be friends first.
BEATRICE	You dare easier be friends with me than fight with mine enemy.
BENEDICK	Is Claudio thine enemy?
BEATRICE	Is he not approved in the height a villain that hath slandered, scorned, dishonoured my kinswoman? O that I were a man! What, bear her in hand until they come to take hands, and then, with public accusation, uncovered slander, unmitigated rancour – O God, that I were a man! I would eat his heart in the market-place.
BENEDICK	Hear me, Beatrice –
BEATRICE	Talk with a man out at a window! A proper saying!
BENEDICK	Nay, but Beatrice –
BEATRICE	Sweet Hero! She is wronged, she is slandered, she is undone.
BENEDICK	Beat –

BEATRICE	Princes and counties! Surely, a princely testimony, a goodly count, Count Comfect – a sweet gallant, surely! o that I were a man for his sake, or that I had any friend would be a man for my sake! But manhood is melted into curtsies, valour into compliment; and men are only turned into tongue, and trim ones too. He is now as valiant as Hercules that only tells a lie and swears it. I cannot be a man with wishing: therefore I will die a woman with grieving.
BENEDICK	Tarry, good Beatrice. By this hand, I love thee.
BEATRICE	Use it for my love some other way than swearing by it.
BENEDICK	Think you in your soul the Count Claudio hath wronged Hero?
BEATRICE	Yea, as sure as I have a thought or a soul.
BENEDICK	Enough: I am engaged. I will challenge him. I will kiss your hand, and so I leave you. By this hand, Claudio shall render me a dear account. As you hear of me, so think of me. Go, comfort your cousin: I must say she is dead; and so, farewell.

Exeunt

Act 5 Scene 4

BENEDICK	Soft and fair, Friar. Which is Beatrice?
BEATRICE	*(Unmasking)* I answer to that name. What is your will?
BENEDICK	Do not you love me?
BEATRICE	Why no – no more than reason.
BENEDICK	Why, then your uncle and the Prince and Claudio Have been deceived. They swore you did.
BEATRICE	Do not you love me?
BENEDICK	Troth, no – no more than reason.
BEATRICE	Why, then my cousin, Margaret and Ursula Are much deceived: for they did swear you did.
BENEDICK	They swore that you were almost sick for me.
BEATRICE	They swore that you were well-nigh dead for me.
BENEDICK	'Tis no such matter. Then you do not love me?
BEATRICE	No, truly, but in friendly recompense.
LEONATO	Come, cousin, I am sure you love the gentleman.
CLAUDIO	And I'll be sworn upon't that he loves her; For here's a paper written in his hand, A halting sonnet of his own pure brain, Fashioned to Beatrice.
HERO	And here's another, Writ in my cousin's hand, stolen from her pocket, Containing her affection unto Benedick.
BENEDICK	A miracle! Here's our own hands against our hearts. Come, I will have thee: but, by this light, I take thee for pity.

BEATRICE   I would not deny you; but, by this good day, I yield
            upon great persuasion – and partly to save your life,
            for I was told you were in a consumption.

BENEDICK   Peace! I will stop your mouth. *(Kissing her)*

                          END OF TEST

Set

A

KEY STAGE 3
Levels 4–7

Shakespeare
Test Paper

English

Romeo and Juliet

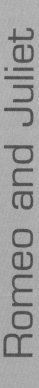

Shakespeare Test Paper

Romeo and Juliet

Instructions:

- find a quiet place where you can sit down and complete the test paper undisturbed

- make sure you have all the necessary equipment to complete the test paper

- read the question carefully

- answer the question on lined paper

- go through and check your answer when you have finished writing

Time:

This test paper is **45 minutes** long.

Check how you have done using pages 123–124 of the Answers and Mark Scheme.

	Max. Mark	**Actual Mark**
Score	18	....

First name ....

Last name ....

Romeo and Juliet

You should spend about 45 minutes on this section.

Romeo and Juliet

In these scenes, the audience see Romeo in different situations.

What do we learn about Romeo in these two scenes?

Support your ideas by referring to both of the extracts which are printed on the following pages.

(18 marks)

Use the printed scenes to answer the question set on page 36.

Act 1 Scene 1

ROMEO	Ay me, sad hours seem long. Was that my father that went hence so fast?	155
BENVOLIO	It was. What sadness lengthens Romeo's hours?	
ROMEO	Not having that which, having, makes them short.	
BENVOLIO	In love?	
ROMEO	Out –	160
BENVOLIO	Of love?	
ROMEO	Out of her favour where I am in love.	
BENVOLIO	Alas, that Love, so gentle in his view, Should be so tyrannous and rough in proof!	
ROMEO	Alas, that Love, whose view is muffled still, Should without eyes see pathways to his will! Where shall we dine? O me! What fray was here? Yet tell me not, for I have heard it all. Here's much to do with hate, but more with love. Why then, O brawling love, O loving hate, O anything of nothing first create! O heavy lightness, serious vanity, Misshapen chaos of well-seeming forms! Feather of lead, bright smoke, cold fire, sick health, Still-waking sleep, that is not what it is! This love feel I, that feel no love in this. Dost thou not laugh?	165 170 175
BENVOLIO	No, coz, I rather weep.	
ROMEO	Good heart, at what?	
BENVOLIO	At *thy* good heart's oppression.	
ROMEO	Why, such is love's transgression. Griefs of mine own lie heavy in my breast, Which thou wilt propagate to have it pressed With more of thine. This love that thou hast shown Doth add more grief to too much of mine own.	180

Love is a smoke made with the fume of sighs:
Being purged, a fire sparkling in lovers' eyes;   185
Being vexed, a sea nourished with loving tears.
What is it else? A madness most discreet,
A choking gall, and a preserving sweet.
Farewell, my coz.

BENVOLIO   Soft, I will go along –
And if you leave me so, you do me wrong.   190

ROMEO   Tut, I have lost myself. I am not here.
This is not Romeo: he's some other where.

BENVOLIO   Tell me in sadness, who is that you love?

ROMEO   What, shall I groan and tell thee?

BENVOLIO   Groan? Why no –
But sadly tell me who.   195

ROMEO   Bid a sick man in sadness make his will –
A word ill urged to one that is so ill.
In sadness, cousin, I do love a woman.

BENVOLIO   I aimed so near when I supposed you loved.

ROMEO   A right good mark-man! And she's fair I love.   200

BENVOLIO   A right fair mark, fair coz, is soonest hit.

ROMEO   Well, in that hit you miss. She'll not be hit
With Cupid's arrow. She hath Dian's wit,
And in strong proof of chastity well-armed,
From Love's weak childish bow she lives uncharmed.   205
She will not stay the siege of loving terms,
Nor bide th' encounter of assailing eyes,
Nor ope her lap to saint-seducing gold.
O, she is rich in beauty – only poor
That when she dies, with beauty dies her store.   210

BENVOLIO   Then she hath sworn that she will still live chaste?

ROMEO   She hath, and in that sparing makes huge waste,
For beauty, starved with her severity,
Cuts beauty off from all posterity.
She is too fair, too wise, wisely too fair,   215
To merit bliss by making me despair.
She hath forsworn to love, and in that vow
Do I live dead, that live to tell it now.

BENVOLIO	Be ruled by me: forget to think of her.
ROMEO	O, teach me how I should forget to think! 220
BENVOLIO	By giving liberty unto thine eyes:
	Examine other beauties.
ROMEO	'Tis the way
	To call hers – exquisite – in question more.
	These happy masks that kiss fair ladies' brows,
	Being black, puts us in mind they hide the fair. 225
	He that is strucken blind cannot forget
	The precious treasure of his eyesight lost.
	Show me a mistress that is passing fair:
	What doth her beauty serve, but as a note
	Where I may read who passed that passing fair? 230
	Farewell. Thou canst not teach me to forget.
BENVOLIO	I'll pay that doctrine, or else die in debt.

Exeunt.

Act 2 Scene 2

The garden, beside the Capulet house.
ROMEO comes forward (reacting to MERCUTIO's joking).

ROMEO	He jests at scars that never felt a wound.

Enter JULIET, coming to her window-balcony above.
ROMEO, below, sees the light at the window, then realises it is JULIET.

      – But soft! What light through yonder window breaks?
It is the east, and Juliet is the sun.
Arise, fair sun, and kill the envious moon,
Who is already sick and pale with grief   5
That thou her maid art far more fair than she.
Be not her maid, since she is envious:
Her vestal livery is but sick and green,
And none but fools do wear it. Cast it off.
    – It is my lady! – O, it is my love!   10
O that she knew she were!
She speaks – yet she says nothing. What of that?
Her eye discourses. I will answer it.
    – I am too bold. 'Tis not to me she speaks.
Two of the fairest stars in all the heaven,   15
Having some business, do entreat her eyes
To twinkle in their spheres till they return.

What if her eyes were there, they in her head?
The brightness of her cheek would shame those stars
As daylight doth a lamp. Her eyes in heaven   20
Would through the airy region stream so bright
That birds would sing and think it were not night!
See how she leans her cheek upon her hand.
O that I were a glove upon that hand,
That I might touch that cheek!

JULIET   Ay me!
ROMEO   (Aside) She speaks.   25
O speak again, bright angel! – For thou art
As glorious to this night, being o'er my head,
As is a wingèd messenger of heaven
Unto the white-upturnèd wondering eyes
Of mortals that fall back to gaze on him   30
When he bestrides the lazy-pacing clouds,
And sails upon the bosom of the air.

JULIET   O Romeo, Romeo! Wherefore art thou Romeo?
Deny thy father and refuse thy name –
Or if thou wilt not, be but sworn my love   35
And I'll no longer be a Capulet.

ROMEO   (Aside) Shall I hear more, or shall I speak at this?

JULIET   'Tis but thy name that is my enemy.
Thou art myself, though not a Montague.
What's 'Montague'? It is nor hand, nor foot,   40
Nor arm, nor face, nor any other part
Belonging to a man. O, be some other name!
What's in a name? That which we call a rose
By any other word would smell as sweet.
So Romeo would, were he not Romeo called,   45
Retain that dear perfection which he owes
Without that title. Romeo, doff thy name –
And for that name, which is no part of thee,
Take all myself.

ROMEO   I take thee at thy word.
Call me but love, and I'll be new-baptized.   50
Henceforth, I never will be Romeo.

END OF TEST

Reading Test Paper

Monsters

English

Instructions:

- find a quiet place where you can sit down and complete the test paper undisturbed

- make sure you have all the necessary equipment to complete the test paper

- read the questions carefully

- answer all the questions

- go through and check your answers when you have finished the test paper

Time:

This test paper is **1 hour 15 minutes** long.

You have **15 minutes** to read the Reading Material. During this time you are not allowed to refer to the Reading Paper to look at the questions.

You have **1 hour** to write the answers.

Write the answers in this paper, then check how you have done using pages 108–110 of the Answers and Mark Scheme.

Page	50	52	54	Max. **Actual**
				Mark **Mark**
Score	....	....	....	32 ....

First name ....

Last name ....

Monsters

ENTER AT OWN RISK

Contents

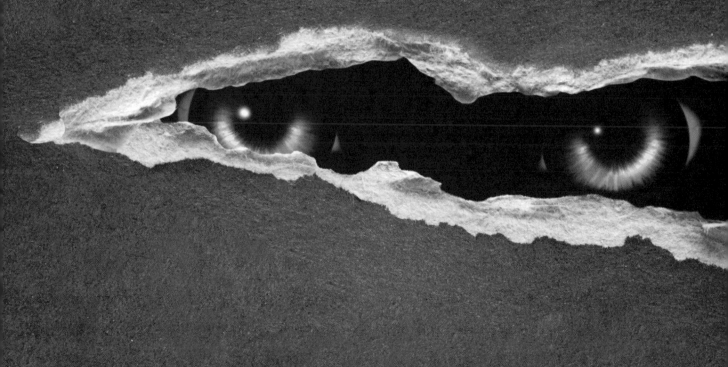

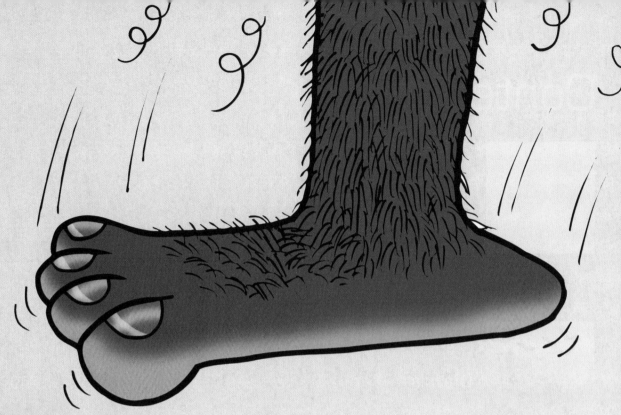

Bigfoot
of North America

1   If the Himalayas of Asia has its Yeti, the Pacific Northwest of
    America has its Bigfoot: a hairy, ape-like, biped that stands
    seven to nine feet tall and weighs between 600
    and 900 pounds.

2   Bigfoot, or as it's often called in Canada, the *Sasquatch*, is mentioned in several
    native American legends. In fact, the term "Sasquatch" is Indian for "hairy
    giant". The first sighting of a Sasquatch footprint by a white man apparently
    came in 1811 near what is now the town of Jasper, Alberta, Canada. A trader
    named David Thompson found some strange footprints, fourteen inches long
    and eight inches wide, with four toes, in the snow.

3   In 1884 the newspaper, *Daily Colonist*, of Victoria, British Columbia,
    told of the capture of a "Sasquatch". The creature was spotted by
    a train crew along the Fraser River. The crew stopped the train,
    gave chase, and captured the animal after following it up a rocky
    hill. The creature was given the name "Jacko" and was
    "… something of the gorilla type, standing four feet seven
    inches in height and weighing 127 pounds. He has long, black,
    strong hair and resembles a human being, with one exception –

his entire body, excepting his hands (or paws) and feet, are covered with glossy hair about one inch long … he possesses extraordinary strength, as he will take hold of a stick and break it by wrenching it or twisting it, which no man could break in the same way."

4   The description of Jacko is so much like that of a chimpanzee, and so unlike later Bigfoot reports, that some have suggested the animal actually was a chimpanzee. If brought back by a sailor from Africa, the animal might have escaped or been turned loose. There is also the strong possibility that the entire story was a hoax. Newspapers of that era often printed hoax stories to amuse their readers (perhaps not unlike some tabloids sold today).

5   Rumours about the Sasquatch continued through the end of the century. Then, in 1910, the murder of two miners, found with their heads cut off, was attributed to the creatures, though there was little supporting evidence that the killing wasn't human in origin. In any case, the place of the murders, Nahanni Valley, in Canada, was changed to Headless Valley, because of the incident.

6   Interest in Bigfoot began to pick up in the United States in 1958 when a bulldozer operator named Jerry Crew found enormous footprints around where he was working in Humboldt County, California. Crew made a cast of the footprint. A local newspaper ran the story of Crew and his footprint with a photo. The story was picked up by other papers and ran throughout the country. It was the picture of Crew holding the "Bigfoot" that made the name stick.

7   In 1967 Roger Patterson and Bob Gimlin, Bigfoot buffs, announced they'd captured Bigfoot with a movie camera. They filmed a few seconds of an ape-like creature, apparently female, moving across a clearing near Bluff Creek in northern California. While the film is not perfectly clear, there is no mistaking the creature in the film for a common animal. The movie shows either a real Bigfoot, or a man in a clever costume. Nobody has ever proved the film fake, though some viewers were suspicious about the unnatural stride the creature had. One scientist who viewed the film, John Napier, of the Smithsonian Institution, admitted, "I couldn't see the zipper, and I still can't."

8   Scientists have a right to be suspicious of Bigfoot evidence. Two known hoax films exist. A controversial carcass, the "Minnesota Iceman", was thought to be a hoax, too. In addition, hoax footprints have been made from fake wooden feet and altered boots. One company even produced a set of oversized plastic strap-on feet that you could use to fool your friends and family.

With kind permission of Lee Krystek © Lee Krystek
unmuseum.org/bigfoot.htm

Dracula

1   **I** stood in silence where I was, for I did not know what to do. Of bell or knocker there was no sign. Through these frowning walls and dark window openings it was not likely that my voice could penetrate. The time I waited seemed endless, and I felt doubts and fears crowding upon me. What sort of place had I come to, and among what kind of people? What sort of grim adventure was it on which I had embarked? Was this a customary incident in the life of a solicitor's clerk sent out to explain the purchase of a London estate to a foreigner? Solicitor's clerk! Mina would not like that. Solicitor, for just before leaving London I got word that my examination was successful, and I am now a full-blown solicitor! I began to rub my eyes and pinch myself to see if I were awake. It all seemed like a horrible nightmare to me, and I expected that I should suddenly awake, and find myself at home, with the dawn struggling in through the windows, as I had now and again felt in the morning after a day of overwork. But my flesh answered the pinching test, and my eyes were not to be deceived. I was indeed awake and among the Carpathians. All I could do now was to be patient, and to wait the coming of morning.

2   Just as I had come to this conclusion I heard a heavy step approaching behind the great door, and saw through the chinks the gleam of a coming light. Then there was the sound of rattling chains and the clanking of massive bolts drawn back. A key was turned with the loud grating noise of long disuse, and the great door swung back.

3   Within, stood a tall old man, clean shaven save for a long white moustache, and clad in black from head to foot, without a single speck of colour about him anywhere. He held in his hand an antique silver lamp, in which the flame burned without a chimney or globe of any kind, throwing long quivering shadows as it flickered in the draught of the open door. The old man motioned me in with his right hand with a courtly gesture, saying in excellent English, but with a strange intonation.

"Welcome   to   my   house!   Enter   freely   and   of   your   own   free   will!"

4   He made no motion of stepping to meet me, but stood like a statue, as though his gesture of welcome had fixed him into stone. The instant, however, that I had stepped over the threshold, he moved impulsively forward, and holding out his hand grasped mine with a strength which made me wince, an effect which was not lessened by the fact that it seemed cold as ice, more like the hand of a dead than a living man.

From Chapter 2 of *Dracula* by Bram Stoker

The Loch Ness Monster

1   The Loch Ness Monster is supposedly living in Scotland's Loch (Lake) Ness. "Nessie", as she is called, is the best known cryptozoological creature in the world.

2   Carvings of this unidentified animal, made by the ancient inhabitants of the Scottish Highlands some 1,500 years ago, are the earliest evidence that Loch Ness harbours a strange aquatic creature.

3   The earliest recorded sighting of the Loch Ness Monster was in the biography of St. Columba by Adamnan in the year 565 AD. The monster apparently attacked and killed a man who was swimming in the River Ness.

4   The monster didn't make headlines again until August 27, 1930 when 3 fishermen reported seeing a disturbance in the water. The men watched as a creature 20 feet long approached their boat throwing water in the air. As it passed them, its wake caused their boat to rock violently.

5   The men were convinced that the disturbance was caused by a living creature. Following the story, the newspaper received several letters from people claiming also to have seen a strange creature in the Loch.

6   In 1962, The Loch Ness Investigation Bureau was formed to act as a research organization and clearing house for information about the creature. In the beginning they only conducted research for a few weeks in the year, but by 1964 they established a more permanent presence around the Loch. Eventually the Bureau established camera stations with both still and cinema cameras with telephoto lenses. They had vans which served as mobile camera stations, and underwater listening devices. Searches were conducted using hot-air balloons and infrared night-time cameras, sonar scanners and submarines.

7   A great deal of information was discovered about the Loch, but they have yet to produce any concrete evidence of a monster.

8   Loch Ness is located in the north of Scotland and is one of a series of interlinked lochs which run along the Great Glen. The Great Glen is a distinctive incision which runs across the country and represents a large geological fault zone. The interlinking was completed in the 19th century following the completion of the Caledonian Canal.

9   The Great Glen is more than 700 ft (213 m) deep and ice free. It is fed by the Oich and other streams and drained by the Ness to the Moray Firth. It forms part of the Caledonian Canal. By volume, Loch Ness is the largest freshwater lake in Great Britain.

10 Since December 1933, when newspapers published accounts of a "monster", 40 to 50 ft (12–15 m) long, said to have been seen in the Loch, there have been alleged sightings.

11 As a result of the publicity, Loch Ness has become a major tourist attraction.

12 Several scientific studies have been conducted, including thorough sonar surveys of the Loch, and these have not revealed any presence of such a "monster".

13 Many people believe that the size and great depth of the Loch, together with potential underwater caves, gives the monster many places to hide.

14 Most of the Nessie witnesses describe something with two humps, a tail, and a snake-like head. A V-shape was often mentioned, as well as a gaping red mouth and horns or antennae on the top of the creature's head. Nessie's movements have been studied, and the films and photos analysed to determine what Nessie might be, if she exists.

15 There are numerous theories as to Nessie's identity, including a snake-like primitive whale known as a zeuglodon, a type of long-necked aquatic seal, giant eels, walruses, floating mats of plants, giant molluscs, otters, a "paraphysical" entity, mirages, and diving birds, but many lake monster researchers seem to favour the plesiosaur theory. The case has occasionally been supported by indistinct photographic evidence – though – in 1994 – a famous 1934 photograph was revealed to be a hoax.

Reproduced with thanks to Crystalinks (http://www.crystalinks.com)

1 From paragraphs one and two, give two features of Bigfoot. *(2 marks)*

□ Q1

i _____

ii _____

2 a) In paragraph two, what does the word "apparently" suggest in this sentence –
   "*The first sighting of a Sasquatch by a white man apparently came in 1811*"? *(1 mark)*

□ Q2a

The word "apparently" suggests _____

_____

   b) In paragraph two, why does the writer refer to "*strange footprints*"? *(1 mark)*

□ Q2b

_____

_____

_____

3 a) Here are the topics of the first four paragraphs. Match up the topic with the correct
   paragraph number. *(2 marks)*

□ Q3a

Topic	Paragraph Number
A description of a captured Sasquatch	
An introduction to what Bigfoot is	
An explanation of what the captured Sasquatch might have been	
The first sightings of a Sasquatch	

   b) Explain why the text has quotations about personal experiences as well as dates and facts. *(1 mark)*

□ Q3b

_____

_____

_____

4   How does the writer make you feel that Bigfoot is probably a fake? You should comment on
the effect of:

- the historical examples chosen

- the writer's comments on those examples

- the language used by the writer.   *(5 marks)*

_____

_____

_____

_____

_____

_____

_____

_____

_____

_____

_____

_____

_____

_____

_____

_____

_____

_____

5 a) From the first sentence, write down the phrase that shows the writer is confused.

(1 mark)

Q5a

_____

_____

_____

   b) How does this phrase help to keep the reader's interest?   *(1 mark)*

Q5b

_____

_____

_____

6 In the first paragraph, the writer describes *"these frowning walls and dark window openings"*.
What does the word "frowning" suggest about the walls?   *(1 mark)*

Q6

_____

_____

_____

7 a) From paragraph three, identify one thing about the old man that suggests he is well-mannered.

(1 mark)

Q7a

_____

_____

_____

   b) From paragraph four, identify one thing about the old man that suggests he is unusual
or strange.   *(1 mark)*

Q7b

_____

_____

_____

8   a) Paragraphs one and two and paragraphs three and four are about different characters and are
        written in different styles.

        Explain one difference in the way that they are written.   *(1 mark)*

        _____

        _____

        _____

        _____

        _____

    b) Explain how the fact that we don't know the old man's name at this point, or who he is, makes
        the story interesting.   *(1 mark)*

        _____

        _____

        _____

        _____

        _____

9   What do you learn about the writer's viewpoint and purpose from the passage? Show whether
        the following statements are TRUE or FALSE by writing T for TRUE or F for FALSE in each of
        the boxes.   *(2 marks)*

        The writer wants us to feel that the narrator is confident.   ☐

        The writer's aim is to entertain and interest the reader.   ☐

        The writer wants us to like the old man.   ☐

        The aim of the writer is to build up tension in the reader.   ☐

10 In the first two paragraphs, the writer gets the reader interested straight away by creating a feeling of mystery.

Find two examples of where the writer does this and explain how each one makes the article mysterious.   *(2 marks)*

Q10

i _____

_____

ii _____

_____

11 In paragraph five (from *"The men …"* to *"..in the Loch."*) the writer tries to make the reader feel that there might be some truth in the monster stories. Choose two different words or phrases and explain how they create this effect on the reader.   *(2 marks)*

Q11

Word/Phrase	Effect on the reader	How it creates this effect on the reader
	makes the reader think that there might be some truth in the monster stories	because it suggests
	makes the reader think that there might be some truth in the monster stories	because it suggests

12 a) In paragraph twelve, it says *"Several scientific studies have been conducted, including thorough sonar surveys of the Loch, and these have not revealed any presence of such a "monster".*
Why does the writer use the word "thorough" in this sentence?   *(1 mark)*

Q12a

_____

_____

b) Why is the word "monster" in inverted commas?   *(1 mark)*

Q12b

_____

_____

13   In this article, how does the writer use language and content to create a serious account about the monster?

You should comment on how the choice of content and language:

- makes the article sound scientific

- makes the article sound well researched

- includes a sense of mystery.   *(5 marks)*

_____

_____

_____

_____

_____

_____

_____

_____

_____

_____

_____

_____

_____

_____

_____

_____

_____

_____

END OF TEST

Set
B

KEY STAGE 3
Levels 4–7

Writing Test
Paper

English

Writing Test Paper

Monsters

Instructions:

- find a quiet place where you can sit down and complete the test paper undisturbed
- make sure you have all the necessary equipment to complete the test paper
- read the questions carefully
- answer the questions on lined paper
- go through and check your answers when you have finished writing

Time:

This test paper is **1 hour 15 minutes** long.

You should spend **30 minutes** on the short writing task, including planning time.

You should spend **45 minutes** on the long writing task, including planning time.

Write the answers on lined paper, then check how you have done using pages 114–118 of the Answers and Mark Scheme.

Short Writing Task

Strand	Max. Mark	Actual Mark
Sentence structure, punctuation and text organisation	6	
Composition and effect	10	
Spelling	4	

Long Writing Task

Strand	Max. Mark	Actual Mark
Sentence structure and punctuation	8	
Text structure and organisation	8	
Composition and effect	14	

First name ....

Last name ....

Writing Paper – Short Writing Task

Spend about 30 minutes on this section.

> You write ghost stories. You are about to start writing your next novel. The publisher wants you to write a convincing opening for your next story before they give you the money to go ahead and write it in full. The publisher wants you to write just the opening two or three paragraphs to show how you are going to get the reader's attention.

The publisher wants you to:

- Set the scene

- Create the mood

- End on a cliffhanger.

Write your opening, based on the ideas given above.

(20 marks, including 4 for spelling)

Writing Paper – Long Writing Task

Spend about 15 minutes planning your answer and 30 minutes writing.

Over the years, many people have reported sightings of ghosts and other supernatural events, but no one has been able to prove whether ghosts or other supernatural things actually exist or not.

Here are some reasons why people *don't* believe in ghosts and the supernatural.

• There is no scientific evidence to prove they exist.

• Often, they are witnessed by people alone, who could be making things up.

• Many of them have been proven to be fakes.

Here are some reasons why people *do* believe in ghosts and the supernatural.

• If only one of the thousands of cases is true, then they exist.

• There are many things that science cannot explain.

• People who have experienced them have been honest and trustworthy.

A Sunday magazine wants you to write an article arguing the case for and against ghosts existing, before you come to your own opinion. You can use the ideas above and any of your own ideas or examples, if you wish.

Write the article.

(30 marks)

END OF TEST

Set
B

KEY STAGE 3
Levels 4–7

Shakespeare
Test Paper

English

Much Ado About Nothing

Shakespeare Test Paper

Much Ado About Nothing

Instructions:

- find a quiet place where you can sit down and complete the test paper undisturbed

- make sure you have all the necessary equipment to complete the test paper

- read the question carefully

- answer the question on lined paper

- go through and check your answer when you have finished writing

Time:

This test paper is **45 minutes** long.

Check how you have done using pages 119 and 121 of the Answers and Mark Scheme.

	Max. Mark	**Actual Mark**
Score	18	....

First name ....

Last name ....

Much Ado About Nothing

You should spend about 45 minutes on this section.

Much Ado About Nothing

In these two scenes we learn a lot about the way that love shows itself.

What do the audience learn about love from these two scenes?

Support your ideas by referring to both of the extracts which are printed on the following pages.

(18 marks)

Use the printed scenes to answer the question set on page 60.

Act 4 Scene 1

All exit except BENEDICK and BEATRICE.

BENEDICK	Lady Beatrice, have you wept all this while?
BEATRICE	Yea, and I will weep a while longer.
BENEDICK	I will not desire that.
BEATRICE	You have no reason: I do it freely.
BENEDICK	Surely I do believe your fair cousin is wronged.
BEATRICE	Ah, how much might the man deserve of me that would right her!
BENEDICK	Is there any way to show such friendship?
BEATRICE	A very even way, but no such friend.
BENEDICK	May a man do it?
BEATRICE	It is a man's office, but not yours.
BENEDICK	I do love nothing in the world so well as you. Is not that strange?
BEATRICE	As strange as the thing I know not. It were as possible for me to say I loved nothing so well as you. But believe me not, and yet I lie not: I confess nothing, nor I deny nothing. I am sorry for my cousin.
BENEDICK	By my sword, Beatrice, thou lovest me.
BEATRICE	Do not swear and eat it.
BENEDICK	I will swear by it that you love me; and I will make him eat it that says I love not you.
BEATRICE	Will you not eat your word?
BENEDICK	With no sauce that can be devised to it. I protest I love thee.

BEATRICE	Why, then, God forgive me!
BENEDICK	What offence, sweet Beatrice?
BEATRICE	You have stayed me in a happy hour. I was about to protest I loved *you*.
BENEDICK	And do it with all thy heart.
BEATRICE	I love you with so much of my heart that none is left to protest.
BENEDICK	Come, bid me do anything for thee.
BEATRICE	Kill Claudio.
BENEDICK	Ha! Not for the wide world.

Act 5 Scene 4

DON PEDRO   How dost thou, Benedick the married man?

BENEDICK   I'll tell thee what, Prince; a college of
wit-crackers cannot flout me out of my humour. Dost
thou think I care for a satire or an epigram? No:
if a man will be beaten with brains, a' shall wear
nothing handsome about him. In brief, since I do
purpose to marry, I will think nothing to any
purpose that the world can say against it; and
therefore never flout at me for what I have said
against it; for man is a giddy thing, and this is my
conclusion. For thy part, Claudio, I did think to
have beaten thee, but in that thou art like to be my
kinsman, live unbruised, and love my cousin.

CLAUDIO   I had well hoped thou wouldst have denied Beatrice,
that I might have cudgelled thee out of thy single
life, to make thee a double-dealer; which, out of
question, thou wilt be, if my cousin do not look
exceedingly narrowly to thee.

BENEDICK   Come, come, we are friends. Let's have a dance ere
we are married, that we may lighten our own hearts
and our wives' heels.

LEONATO   We'll have dancing afterward.

BENEDICK   First, of my word! Therefore play, music. Prince,
thou art sad; get thee a wife, get thee a wife!
There is no staff more reverend than one tipped with horn.

Enter a Messenger

Messenger   My lord, your brother John is ta'en in flight,
And brought with armed men back to Messina.

BENEDICK   Think not on him till to-morrow:
I'll devise thee brave punishments for him.
Strike up, pipers.
                    (Dance)

Exeunt

END OF TEST

Set

B

KEY STAGE 3
Levels 4–7

Shakespeare
Test Paper

English

Shakespeare Test Paper

Romeo and Juliet

Instructions:

- find a quiet place where you can sit down and complete the test paper undisturbed

- make sure you have all the necessary equipment to complete the test paper

- read the question carefully

- answer the question on lined paper

- go through and check your answer when you have finished writing

Time:

This test paper is **45 minutes** long.

Check how you have done using pages 123 and 125 of the Answers and Mark Scheme.

	Max. Mark	**Actual Mark**
Score	18	....

First name ....

Last name ....

Romeo and Juliet

Romeo and Juliet

You should spend about 45 minutes on this section.

Romeo and Juliet

In these scenes, Romeo thinks that, and behaves like, he is in love.

What do we learn about lovers' behaviour in these scenes?

Support your ideas by referring to both of the extracts which are printed on the following pages.

(18 marks)

Use the printed scenes to answer the question set on page 67.

Act 1 Scene 1

LADY MONTAGUE	O where is Romeo? Saw you him today? Right glad I am he was not at this fray.	110
BENVOLIO	Madam, an hour before the worshipped sun Peered forth the golden window of the east, A troubled mind drove me to walk abroad – Where, underneath the grove of sycamore That westward rooteth from this city side, So early walking did I see your son. Towards him I made, but he was ware of me, And stole into the covert of the wood. I, measuring his affections by my own, Which then most sought where most might not be found, Being one too many by my weary self, Pursued my humour not pursuing his, And gladly shunned who gladly fled from me.	115 120
MONTAGUE	Many a morning hath he there been seen, With tears augmenting the fresh morning's dew, Adding to clouds more clouds with his deep sighs. But all so soon as the all-cheering sun Should in the farthest east begin to draw The shady curtains from Aurora's bed, Away from light steals home my heavy son, And private in his chamber pens himself, Shuts up his windows, locks fair daylight out, And makes himself an artificial night. Black and portentous must this humour prove, Unless good counsel may the cause remove.	125 130 135
BENVOLIO	My noble uncle, do you know the cause?	
MONTAGUE	I neither know it, nor can learn of him.	
BENVOLIO	Have you importuned him by any means?	
MONTAGUE	Both by myself and many other friends: But he, his own affections' counsellor, Is to himself – I will not say how true – But to himself so secret and so close, So far from sounding and discovery As is the bud bit with an envious worm Ere he can spread his sweet leaves to the air, Or dedicate his beauty to the sun. Could we but learn from whence his sorrows grow, We would as willingly give cure as know.	140 145

BENVOLIO	See where he comes. So please you, step aside.	150
	I'll know his grievance or be much denied.	

MONTAGUE   I would thou wert so happy by thy stay
To hear true shrift. Come, madam, let's away.

Exit MONTAGUE, with LADY MONTAGUE.

BENVOLIO   Good morrow, cousin.

ROMEO   Is the day so young?

BENVOLIO   But new struck nine.

ROMEO   Ay me, sad hours seem long.   155
Was that my father that went hence so fast?

BENVOLIO   It was. What sadness lengthens Romeo's hours?

ROMEO   Not having that which, having, makes them short.

BENVOLIO   In love?

ROMEO   Out –   160

BENVOLIO   Of love?

ROMEO   Out of her favour where I am in love.

BENVOLIO   Alas, that Love, so gentle in his view,
Should be so tyrannous and rough in proof!

ROMEO   Alas, that Love, whose view is muffled still,   165
Should without eyes see pathways to his will!
Where shall we dine? O me! What fray was here?
Yet tell me not, for I have heard it all.
Here's much to do with hate, but more with love.
Why then, O brawling love, O loving hate,   170
O anything of nothing first create!
O heavy lightness, serious vanity,
Misshapen chaos of well-seeming forms!
Feather of lead, bright smoke, cold fire, sick health,
Still-waking sleep, that is not what it is!   175
This love feel I, that feel no love in this.
Dost thou not laugh?

BENVOLIO   No, coz, I rather weep.

Act 2 Scene 2

JULIET	What man art thou, that thus bescreened in night So stumblest on my counsel?
ROMEO	By a name I know not how to tell thee who I am. My name, dear saint, is hateful to myself 55 Because it is an enemy to thee. Had I it written, I would tear the word.
JULIET	My ears have yet not drunk a hundred words Of thy tongue's uttering, yet I know the sound. Art thou Romeo, and a Montague? 60
ROMEO	Neither, fair maid, if either thee dislike.
JULIET	How cam'st thou hither, tell me, and wherefore? The orchard walls are high and hard to climb – And the place death, considering who thou art, If any of my kinsmen find thee here. 65
ROMEO	With love's light wings did I o'erperch these walls, For stony limits cannot hold love out – And what love can do, that dares love attempt. Therefore thy kinsmen are no stop to me.
JULIET	If they do see thee, they will murder thee. 70
ROMEO	Alack, there lies more peril in thine eye Than twenty of their swords. Look thou but sweet And I am proof against their enmity.
JULIET	I would not for the world they saw thee here.
ROMEO	I have night's cloak to hide me from their eyes. 75 And but thou love me, *let* them find me here. My life were better ended by their hate Than death proroguèd, wanting of thy love.
JULIET	By whose direction found'st thou out this place?
ROMEO	By love, that first did prompt me to inquire. 80 He lent me counsel, and I lent him eyes. I am no pilot, yet wert thou as far As that vast shore washed with the farthest sea, I should adventure for such merchandise.
JULIET	Thou knowest the mask of night is on my face, 85 Else would a maiden blush bepaint my cheek For that which thou hast heard me speak tonight. Fain would I dwell on form – fain, fain deny What I have spoke. – But farewell compliment!

Dost thou love me? I know thou wilt say 'Ay' –   90
And I will take thy word. Yet if thou swear'st
Thou mayst prove false. At lovers' perjuries
They say Jove laughs. O gentle Romeo,
If thou dost love, pronounce it faithfully.
Or if thou think I am too quickly won,   95
I'll frown, and be perverse, and say thee nay,
So thou wilt woo – but else, not for the world.
In truth, fair Montague, I am too fond,
And therefore thou mayst think my 'haviour light.
But trust me, gentleman, I'll prove more true   100
Than those that have more cunning to be strange.
I should have been more strange, I must confess,
But that thou overheard'st, ere I was ware,
My true-love passion. Therefore pardon me,
And not impute this yielding to light love,   105
Which the dark night hath so discoverèd.

ROMEO   Lady, by yonder blessèd moon I vow,
That tips with silver all these fruit-tree tops –

JULIET   O swear not by the moon, th' inconstant moon,
That monthly changes in her circled orb,   110
Lest that thy love prove likewise variable.

ROMEO   What shall I swear by?

JULIET   Do not swear at all. –
Or if thou wilt, swear by thy gracious self,
Which is the god of my idolatry,
And I'll believe thee.

ROMEO   If my heart's dear love –   115

JULIET   Well, do not swear. Although I joy in thee,
I have no joy of this contract tonight.
It is too rash, too unadvised, too sudden –
Too like the lightning, which doth cease to be
Ere one can say 'It lightens'. Sweet, good night.   120
This bud of love, by summer's ripening breath,
May prove a beauteous flower when next we meet.
Good night, good night! As sweet repose and rest
Come to thy heart as that within my breast.

ROMEO   O wilt thou leave me so unsatisfied?   125

JULIET   What satisfaction canst thou have tonight?

ROMEO   Th' exchange of thy love's faithful vow for mine.

END OF TEST

Set

C

KEY STAGE 3
Levels 4–7

Reading Test
Paper

English

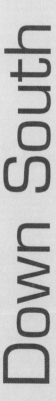

Down South

Reading Test Paper

Down South

Instructions:

- find a quiet place where you can sit down and complete the test paper undisturbed

- make sure you have all the necessary equipment to complete the test paper

- read the questions carefully

- answer all the questions

- go through and check your answers when you have finished the test paper

Time:

This test paper is **1 hour 15 minutes** long.

You have **15 minutes** to read the Reading Material. During this time you are not allowed to refer to the Reading Paper to look at the questions.

You have **1 hour** to write the answers.

Write the answers in this paper, then check how you have done using pages 111–113 of the Answers and Mark Scheme.

Page	81	83	85	Max. Mark	**Actual Mark**
Score	....	....	....	32	....

First name ....

Last name ....

Down South

Contents

Jean Lafitte

1 Jean Lafitte or Laffite (*ca*1780 – *ca*1826?), was a pirate in the Gulf of Mexico in the early 19th century. He established his own "kingdom" of Barataria in the swamps and bayous near New Orleans after the Louisiana Purchase of 1803. He claimed to command more than 1000 men and provided them as troops for the Battle of New Orleans (1815). Afterwards he engaged in the slave trade after it had been banned.

2 Lafitte was a colourful character, said to have been born in France. He engaged in smuggling and privateering, with his "Kingdom of Barataria" (in what is now Louisiana) recognising the sovereignty of no other nation.

3 A controversial manuscript, known as the "Journal" of Jean Laffite, relates how, after his announced death in the 1820s, he lived in several states in the United States, raised a family and wrote this journal. At his request the publication of the journal was delayed for 100 years. In the 1950s the journal was translated from the French language and published. The original manuscript was purchased by Texas Governor Price Daniel and is on display at the Sam Houston Regional Library and Archives in Liberty, Texas.

4 Lafitte claimed never to have plundered an American vessel, and though he engaged in the contraband slave trade, he is accounted as a great romantic figure in Cajun Louisiana. His legend was perpetuated in Cecil B. DeMille's classic, *The Buccaneer* and even by a poem of Byron:

> *He left a corsair's name to other times,*
> *Linked one virtue to a thousand crimes.*

5 After the War of 1812, Lafitte or Laffite was active in the Neutral strip of coast between Spanish Texas and American Louisiana, left unoccupied and lawless until 1821.

6 His later years are obscure; a man many said was Lafitte died in Yucatan.

7 A U.S. National Park is named after him, in six physically separate sites in southeastern Louisiana, interpreting the local Acadian culture. The Barataria Preserve (in Jefferson Parish, Louisiana) interprets the natural and cultural history of the uplands, swamps, and marshlands of the region. Six miles southeast of New Orleans is the Chalmette Battlefield and National Cemetery, actual site of the 1815 battle and the final resting place for soldiers from the Civil War, Spanish – American War, World Wars I and II, and Vietnam.

8 **Jean Lafitte** is the name of a Cajun fishing village and tourist spot sited on Bayou Barataria.

With thanks to www.fact-index.com/j/je/jean_lafitte.html

Arriving in

1   They coasted into the delta, breathed its odour of mud and wood smoke under sunset clouds, gold curls combed out of the west, or the powdered stamens of a broad-throated flower. In the dusk they could see flickering lights in the side channels, sometimes hear a gruesome roar – the alligators, said a deckhand; no, a cow bogged in mud, said the woman with the nephews. The immigrants crowded the rail as the quivering ship moved into the Mississippi River, within the pincer of land. Silvano stood next to his father. A red moon crawled out of the east. On the shore the boy heard a horse snort. Hours before New Orleans the odour of the city reached them – a fetid stink of cesspools and the smell of burning sugar.

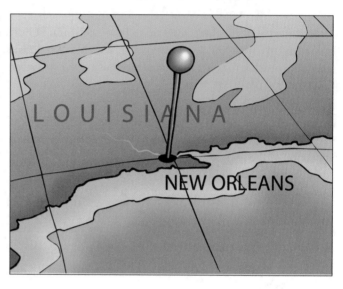

A demon in the backhouse

2   Nothing went as the accordion maker anticipated. The young man from the train was not at the dock. They waited hours for him while the other passengers disappeared into the teeming streets.

3   "True friends are as rare as white flies," said the accordion maker bitterly. Silvano gaped at the black men and especially the women, whose heads were wrapped in turbans as though they concealed emeralds and rubies and chains of gold beneath the winded cloth. They puzzled their way along the noisy, thronged streets with the young man's map and found Decatur Street, but there was no number 16 there, only charred timbers among rampant fireweed, a gap in the row of frowsty tenements. The accordion maker forced his courage, spoke to an approaching man who looked Sicilian; at least his hair appeared Sicilian.

4   "Excuse me, I seek a boardinghouse, number sixteen, but it seems there is no building here – " The man did not answer, spat to his right as he passed. Silvano saw the punishment for not knowing American. The man must be American – one who despised Sicilians ...

New Orleans

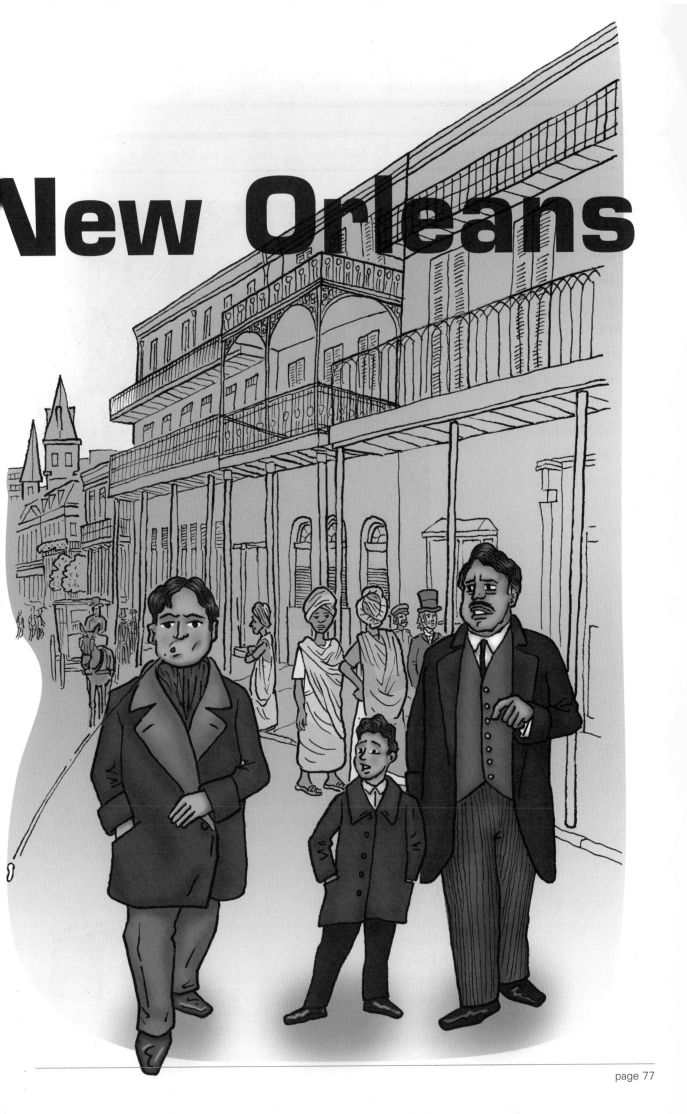

Back Forward Stop Refresh Home AutoFill Print Mail

Address: @ www.lonelyplanet.com

@ Live Home Page @ Apple @ Apple Support @ Apple Store @ .Mac @ Mac OS X @ Microsoft MacTopia

Favorites History Search Scrapbook Page Holder

New Orleans

1 New Orleans seduces with Caribbean colour and waves of sultry southern heat. Enshrouding us in dreams and ancient melodies, its sweet-tasting cocktails are laced with voodoo potions. The unofficial state motto, *laissez les bons temps rouler* ("let the good times roll"), pretty much says it all.

2 Called by some "The City That Care Forgot," New Orleans has a well-earned reputation for excess and debauchery. It's a cultural gumbo of African, Indian, Cajun and Creole influences. Whether you're looking for history, drama and intrigue or just a damn good bop in the street, New Orleans is it.

Area: 468 sq km
Population: 1.2 million
Country: USA
Time Zone: GMT/UTC -6 (Central Time)
Telephone Area Code: 504

BACK TO TOP

3   At the big toe of boot-shaped Louisiana, New Orleans nestles between Lake Pontchartrain, a huge but shallow body of saltwater that forms the northern edge of town, and a meniscus-shaped bend of the Mississippi River, about 145 river kilometres (90 miles) above where it empties into the Gulf of Mexico. The original and most visited portions of the city parallel the northern riverbank. Directions upriver or downriver are relative to the water flow, which bends maddeningly to all points of the compass. The Mississippi and Lake Pontchartrain also provide "riverside" or "lakeside" orientation.

4   New Orleans comprises a checkerboard of neighborhoods of different wealth and ethnicity – it's often only a few steps from ghetto to endowed estates. At the easternmost point of the city's crescent-shaped core is the heart of the original city, the French Quarter. To the southwest, the Uptown area encompasses the Garden District, universities and palatial mansions along the St Charles Ave Streetcar Line, which leads to the Riverbend area at the other end of the crescent.

5   Older *faubourgs* (suburbs) border the crowded French Quarter – to the east, the Faubourg Marigny appeals to a bohemian, mostly gay crowd, while the more down-at-heels Faubourg Tremé to the north is a black neighborhood known for its music. Downriver from Faubourg Marigny is the Bywater, a burgeoning artist hangout in an otherwise marginal district.

6   New Orleans International Airport (MSY) is 18 km (11 miles) west of the city center in Kenner, while both trains and buses share New Orleans Union Passenger Terminal ("Union Station") on Loyola Ave in the Central Business District (CBD), between the French Quarter and the Uptown area.

7   West of New Orleans you'll find the Cajun wetlands, an area of French patois-speaking rural people who still depend on the natural resources of the swamps. The Cajuns' Spanish counterparts, the Isleños, live in the coastal fishing villages south of New Orleans. Upstream along the Mississippi River, antebellum sugar plantations attract visitors who marvel at elegant plantation homes. An occasional slave cabin remains as a reminder of how the wealth was gained.

BACK TO TOP

Used with kind permission of Lonely Planet

> Questions 1–4 are about the "Jean Lafitte" extract on page 75 of the Reading Material.

1   From paragraph one, give two different things that Jean Lafitte was well known for. *(2 marks)*

i _____

ii _____

2   In paragraphs two and four, what does the choice of words in the following phrases suggest about Jean Lafitte?

a) *"Lafitte was a colourful character"*   *(1 mark)*

suggests _____

_____

b) *"he is accounted as a great romantic figure in Cajun Louisiana"*   *(1 mark)*

suggests _____

_____

3   a) The article is split into a number of paragraphs. Each paragraph has a topic. Fill in the table with the missing paragraph numbers.   *(2 marks)*

Topic	Paragraph Number
The end of Jean Lafitte's life	
Two places that exist today, connected to Jean Lafitte	
A summary of Jean Lafitte's main achievements	
The history of a diary about Jean Lafitte	
A place named after Jean Lafitte	
Reasons why Jean Lafitte became famous	

b) Give one reason why the text contains so many facts and very few opinions.   *(1 mark)*

_____

_____

4   How does the writer try to give the reader a fair view of the story of Jean Lafitte? You should
     comment on the effect of:

- the language used to describe Jean Lafitte and his life

- the use of facts and dates

- the content of the writing   *(5 marks)*

5   a) From the sentence at the start of paragraph one, write down one word which suggests that
       the boat is moving slowly but effortlessly.   *(1 mark)*

_____

    b) What does the word "*gruesome*" suggest in paragraph one?   *(1 mark)*

_____

_____

_____

_____

6   In paragraph one, the writer says "*The immigrants crowded the rail as the quivering ship
     moved into the Mississippi River ...*" What does the phrase "*crowded the rail*" suggest about
     the people?   *(1 mark)*

_____

_____

_____

_____

_____

7   From the whole text, identify two bad things about New Orleans.   *(2 marks)*

    i   _____

    _____

    _____

    ii _____

    _____

    _____

8   a) This story is divided by a sub-heading: "*A demon in the backhouse*". Which event has the
        writer chosen to leave out and not describe, where the sub-heading is?   *(1 mark)*

Q8a

_____

_____

    b) Explain how the first paragraph prepares us for the fact that the accordion maker's arrival in
        New Orleans was not going to be easy?   *(1 mark)*

Q8b

_____

_____

_____

_____

_____

_____

9   What do you learn about the writer's viewpoint and purpose from the passage? Show whether
        the following statements are TRUE or FALSE by writing T for TRUE or F for FALSE in each of
        the boxes.   *(2 marks)*

Q9

The writer wants us to be aware that New Orleans is a smelly place.   ☐

The writer wants the reader to feel like the accordion maker.   ☐

The aim of the writer is to scare the reader.   ☐

The aim of the writer is to put people off visiting New Orleans.   ☐

subtotal

10   The web-page begins "*New Orleans seduces with Caribbean colour and waves of sultry southern heat.*"

Explain two ways that this sentence makes the reader want to read more. Support each answer with a quotation from the sentence.   *(2 marks)*

i _____

_____

ii _____

_____

11   Paragraph one, from "*Enshrouding us ...*" to the end of paragraph two, "*New Orleans is it,*" makes us feel that New Orleans is an exciting place but with a darker side. Choose two different words or phrases and explain how they create this effect on the reader.   *(2 marks)*

Word/Phrase	Effect on the reader	How it creates this effect on the reader
	makes the reader think that New Orleans is exciting	because it suggests
	makes the reader think that New Orleans has a darker side	because it suggests

12   In the fourth paragraph, it says "*New Orleans comprises a checkerboard of neighbourhoods of different wealth and ethnicity*".

a) Why is New Orleans compared to a checkerboard?   *(1 mark)*

_____

_____

b) In paragraph five, the word "suburbs" is in brackets. Why?   *(1 mark)*

_____

_____

13   How is language used in the whole text to make New Orleans sound like an exciting place
      to visit?

      You should comment on how the choice of words and phrases:

      •   makes New Orleans sound lively

      •   makes New Orleans sound mysterious

      •   makes New Orleans sound historical and cultured.   (5 marks)

Q13

_____

_____

_____

_____

_____

_____

_____

_____

_____

_____

_____

_____

_____

_____

_____

_____

_____

_____

                              END OF TEST

subtotal

Set

C

KEY STAGE 3
Levels 4–7

Writing Test
Paper

English

Down South

Writing Test Paper

Down South

Instructions:

- find a quiet place where you can sit down and complete the test paper undisturbed
- make sure you have all the necessary equipment to complete the test paper
- read the questions carefully
- answer the questions on lined paper
- go through and check your answers when you have finished writing

Time:

This test paper is **1 hour 15 minutes** long.

You should spend **30 minutes** on the short writing task, including planning time.

You should spend **45 minutes** on the long writing task, including planning time.

Write the answers on lined paper, then check how you have done using pages 114–118 of the Answers and Mark Scheme.

Short Writing Task

Strand	Max. Mark	Actual Mark
Sentence structure, punctuation and text organisation	6	
Composition and effect	10	
Spelling	4	

Long Writing Task

Strand	Max. Mark	Actual Mark
Sentence structure and punctuation	8	
Text structure and organisation	8	
Composition and effect	14	

First name

Last name

Writing Paper – Short Writing Task

Spend about 30 minutes on this section.

You have just returned from a holiday which turned out to be a nightmare. The following things went wrong.

> Your flights were delayed by 30 hours and you had to sleep in the airport lounge.
>
> When you arrived, your rooms had been double-booked and were taken.
>
> All your family got food-poisoning from the hotel's own food.

Write a letter to your local newspaper about what happened.

Analyse what went wrong and comment on the company you used.

You do not need to put any addresses – just start your letter with "Dear Sir or Madam".

Write the letter.

(20 marks, including 4 for spelling)

Writing Paper – Long Writing Task

Spend about 15 minutes planning your answer and 30 minutes writing.

Your local council have allocated a large part of their budget to attracting more tourists to your area. You are the council's publicity officer and it is your job to write the text for the brochure. You need to persuade tourists to visit your area.

In your brochure, you need to do these things.

• Tell people what your area has to offer them.

• Describe your area honestly, but make it sound as good as possible without telling lies!

• Sell your area to those people it might appeal to. Old or young? Single or married?

The council **DO NOT** need you to **design** the brochure – they **just** want you to write the text for it.

Write the text for the brochure.

(30 marks)

END OF TEST

Set

C

KEY STAGE 3
Levels 4–7

Shakespeare
Test Paper

English

Shakespeare Test Paper

Much Ado About Nothing

Instructions:

- find a quiet place where you can sit down and complete the test paper undisturbed

- make sure you have all the necessary equipment to complete the test paper

- read the question carefully

- answer the question on lined paper

- go through and check your answer when you have finished writing

Time:

This test paper is **45 minutes** long.

Check how you have done using pages 119 and 122 of the Answers and Mark Scheme.

	Max. Mark	**Actual Mark**
Score	18	....

First name ....

Last name ....

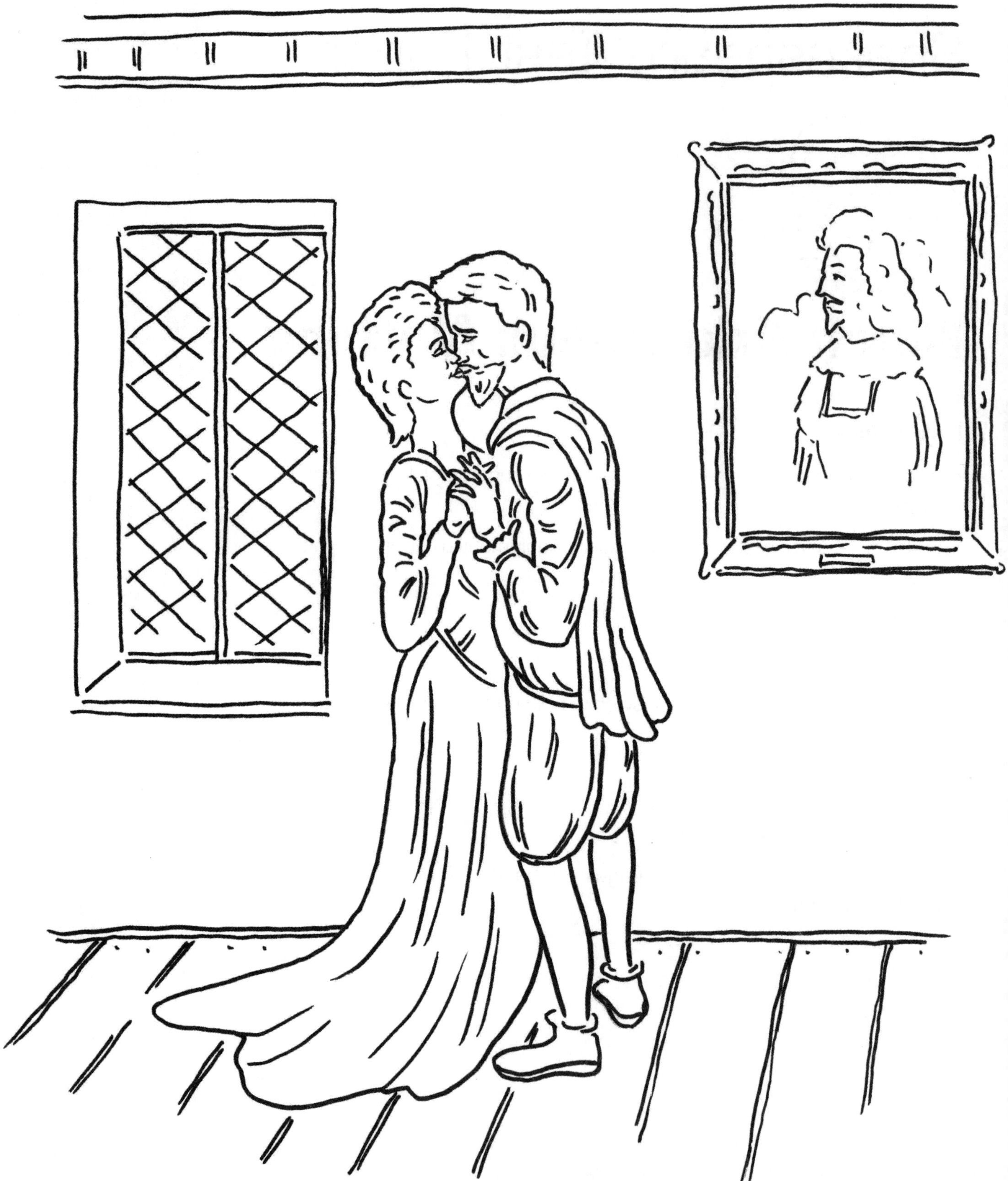

Much Ado About Nothing

You should spend about 45 minutes on this section.

Much Ado About Nothing

In these two scenes we learn about the relationships of key characters in the play.

What do we learn about relationships in these scenes?

Support your ideas by referring to both of the extracts which are printed on the following pages.

(18 marks)

Use the printed scenes to answer the question set on page 91.

Act 4 Scene 1

BENEDICK	Come, bid me do anything for thee.
BEATRICE	Kill Claudio.
BENEDICK	Ha! Not for the wide world.
BEATRICE	You kill me to deny it. Farewell.
BENEDICK	Tarry, sweet Beatrice.
BEATRICE	I am gone though I am here. There is no love in you. Nay, I pray you, let me go.
BENEDICK	Beatrice –
BEATRICE	In faith, I will go.
BENEDICK	We'll be friends first.
BEATRICE	You dare easier be friends with me than fight with mine enemy.
BENEDICK	Is Claudio thine enemy?
BEATRICE	Is he not approved in the height a villain that hath slandered, scorned, dishonoured my kinswoman? O that I were a man! What, bear her in hand until they come to take hands, and then, with public accusation, uncovered slander, unmitigated rancour – O God, that I were a man! I would eat his heart in the market-place.
BENEDICK	Hear me, Beatrice –
BEATRICE	Talk with a man out at a window! A proper saying!
BENEDICK	Nay, but Beatrice –
BEATRICE	Sweet Hero! She is wronged, she is slandered, she is undone.
BENEDICK	Beat –

BEATRICE	Princes and counties! Surely, a princely testimony, a goodly count, Count Comfect – a sweet gallant, surely! O that I were a man for his sake, or that I had any friend would be a man for my sake! But manhood is melted into curtsies, valour into compliment; and men are only turned into tongue, and trim ones too. He is now as valiant as Hercules that only tells a lie and swears it. I cannot be a man with wishing: therefore I will die a woman with grieving.
BENEDICK	Tarry, good Beatrice. By this hand, I love thee.
BEATRICE	Use it for my love some other way than swearing by it.
BENEDICK	Think you in your soul the Count Claudio hath wronged Hero?
BEATRICE	Yea, as sure as I have a thought or a soul.
BENEDICK	Enough: I am engaged. I will challenge him. I will kiss your hand, and so I leave you. By this hand, Claudio shall render me a dear account. As you hear of me, so think of me. Go, comfort your cousin: I must say she is dead; and so, farewell.

Exeunt.

Act 5 Scene 4

BENEDICK	Soft and fair, Friar. Which is Beatrice?
BEATRICE	*(Unmasking)* I answer to that name. What is your will?
BENEDICK	Do not you love me?
BEATRICE	Why no – no more than reason.
BENEDICK	Why, then your uncle and the Prince and Claudio Have been deceived. They swore you did.
BEATRICE	Do not you love me?
BENEDICK	Troth, no – no more than reason.
BEATRICE	Why, then my cousin Margaret and Ursula Are much deceived: for they did swear you did.
BENEDICK	They swore that you were almost sick for me.
BEATRICE	They swore that you were well-nigh dead for me.
BENEDICK	'Tis no such matter. Then you do not love me?
BEATRICE	No, truly, but in friendly recompense.
LEONATO	Come, cousin, I am sure you love the gentleman.
CLAUDIO	And I'll be sworn upon't that he loves her; For here's a paper written in his hand, A halting sonnet of his own pure brain, Fashioned to Beatrice.
HERO	And here's another, Writ in my cousin's hand, stolen from her pocket, Containing her affection unto Benedick.
BENEDICK	A miracle! Here's our own hands against our hearts. Come, I will have thee: but, by this light, I take thee for pity.

BEATRICE   I would not deny you; but, by this good day, I yield
                  upon great persuasion – and partly to save your life,
                  for I was told you were in a consumption.

BENEDICK   Peace! I will stop your mouth. *(Kissing her)*

END OF TEST

Set

C

KEY STAGE 3
Levels 4–7

Shakespeare
Test Paper

English

Romeo and Juliet

Shakespeare Test Paper

Romeo and Juliet

Instructions:

- find a quiet place where you can sit down and complete the test paper undisturbed

- make sure you have all the necessary equipment to complete the test paper

- read the question carefully

- answer the question on lined paper

- go through and check your answer when you have finished writing

Time:

This test paper is **45 minutes** long.

Check how you have done using pages 123 and 126 of the Answers and Mark Scheme.

	Max. Mark	**Actual Mark**
Score	18	....

First name ....

Last name ....

Romeo and Juliet

You should spend about 45 minutes on this section.

Romeo and Juliet

In these scenes, other characters give their opinions on Romeo.

What do we learn about attitudes towards Romeo in these scenes?

Support your ideas by referring to both of the extracts which are printed on the following pages.

(18 marks)

Use the printed scenes to answer the question set on page 98.

Act 1 Scene 1

| LADY MONTAGUE | O where is Romeo? Saw you him today? | 110 |
| | Right glad I am he was not at this fray. | |

BENVOLIO	Madam, an hour before the worshipped sun	
	Peered forth the golden window of the east,	
	A troubled mind drove me to walk abroad –	
	Where, underneath the grove of sycamore	115
	That westward rooteth from this city side,	
	So early walking did I see your son.	
	Towards him I made, but he was ware of me,	
	And stole into the covert of the wood.	
	I, measuring his affections by my own,	120
	Which then most sought where most might not be found,	
	Being one too many by my weary self,	
	Pursued my humour not pursuing his,	
	And gladly shunned who gladly fled from me.	

MONTAGUE	Many a morning hath he there been seen,	125
	With tears augmenting the fresh morning's dew,	
	Adding to clouds more clouds with his deep sighs.	
	But all so soon as the all-cheering sun	
	Should in the farthest east begin to draw	
	The shady curtains from Aurora's bed,	130
	Away from light steals home my heavy son,	
	And private in his chamber pens himself,	
	Shuts up his windows, locks fair daylight out,	
	And makes himself an artificial night.	
	Black and portentous must this humour prove,	135
	Unless good counsel may the cause remove.	

| BENVOLIO | My noble uncle, do you know the cause? | |

| MONTAGUE | I neither know it, nor can learn of him. | |

| BENVOLIO | Have you importuned him by any means? | |

MONTAGUE	Both by myself and many other friends:	140
	But he, his own affections' counsellor,	
	Is to himself – I will not say how true –	
	But to himself so secret and so close,	
	So far from sounding and discovery	
	As is the bud bit with an envious worm	145
	Ere he can spread his sweet leaves to the air,	
	Or dedicate his beauty to the sun.	
	Could we but learn from whence his sorrows grow,	
	We would as willingly give cure as know.	

Enter ROMEO.

BENVOLIO	See where he comes. So please you, step aside.
	I'll know his grievance or be much denied.

MONTAGUE I would thou wert so happy by thy stay
To hear true shrift. Come, madam, let's away.

Exit MONTAGUE, with LADY MONTAGUE.

BENVOLIO Good morrow, cousin.

ROMEO   Is the day so young?

BENVOLIO But new struck nine.

ROMEO   Ay me, sad hours seem long.
Was that my father that went hence so fast?

BENVOLIO It was. What sadness lengthens Romeo's hours?

ROMEO Not having that which, having, makes them short.

BENVOLIO In love?

ROMEO Out –

BENVOLIO Of love?

ROMEO Out of her favour where I am in love.

BENVOLIO Alas, that Love, so gentle in his view,
Should be so tyrannous and rough in proof!

150

155

160

Act 2 Scene 2

JULIET What man art thou, that thus bescreened in night
So stumblest on my counsel?

ROMEO   By a name
I know not how to tell thee who I am.
My name, dear saint, is hateful to myself
Because it is an enemy to thee.
Had I it written, I would tear the word.

JULIET My ears have yet not drunk a hundred words
Of thy tongue's uttering, yet I know the sound.
Art thou Romeo, and a Montague?

ROMEO Neither, fair maid, if either thee dislike.

55

60

JULIET	How cam'st thou hither, tell me, and wherefore?	
	The orchard walls are high and hard to climb –	
	And the place death, considering who thou art,	
	If any of my kinsmen find thee here.	65

ROMEO	With love's light wings did I o'erperch these walls,	
	For stony limits cannot hold love out –	
	And what love can do, that dares love attempt.	
	Therefore thy kinsmen are no stop to me.	

JULIET	If they do see thee, they will murder thee.	70

ROMEO	Alack, there lies more peril in thine eye	
	Than twenty of their swords. Look thou but sweet	
	And I am proof against their enmity.	

JULIET	I would not for the world they saw thee here.	

ROMEO	I have night's cloak to hide me from their eyes.	75
	And but thou love me, *let* them find me here.	
	My life were better ended by their hate	
	Than death proroguèd, wanting of thy love.	

JULIET	By whose direction found'st thou out this place?	

ROMEO	By love, that first did prompt me to inquire.	80
	He lent me counsel, and I lent him eyes.	
	I am no pilot, yet wert thou as far	
	As that vast shore washed with the farthest sea,	
	I should adventure for such merchandise.	

JULIET	Thou knowest the mask of night is on my face,	85
	Else would a maiden blush bepaint my cheek	
	For that which thou hast heard me speak tonight.	
	Fain would I dwell on form – fain, fain deny	
	What I have spoke. – But farewell compliment!	
	Dost thou love me? I know thou wilt say 'Ay' –	90
	And I will take thy word. Yet if thou swear'st	
	Thou mayst prove false. At lovers' perjuries	
	They say Jove laughs. O gentle Romeo,	
	If thou dost love, pronounce it faithfully.	
	Or if thou think I am too quickly won,	95
	I'll frown, and be perverse, and say thee nay,	
	So thou wilt woo – but else, not for the world.	
	In truth, fair Montague, I am too fond,	
	And therefore thou mayst think my 'haviour light.	
	But trust me, gentleman, I'll prove more true	100
	Than those that have more cunning to be strange.	
	I should have been more strange, I must confess,	
	But that thou overheard'st, ere I was ware,	
	My true-love passion. Therefore pardon me,	
	And not impute this yielding to light love,	105
	Which the dark night hath so discoverèd.	

ROMEO	Lady, by yonder blessèd moon I vow,
	That tips with silver all these fruit-tree tops –

JULIET	O swear not by the moon, th' inconstant moon,	
	That monthly changes in her circled orb,	110
	Lest that thy love prove likewise variable.	

ROMEO   What shall I swear by?

JULIET   Do not swear at all. –
Or if thou wilt, swear by thy gracious self,
Which is the god of my idolatry,
And I'll believe thee.

ROMEO   If my heart's dear love –   115

JULIET   Well, do not swear. Although I joy in thee,
I have no joy of this contract tonight.
It is too rash, too unadvised, too sudden –
Too like the lightning, which doth cease to be
Ere one can say 'It lightens'. Sweet, good night.   120
This bud of love, by summer's ripening breath,
May prove a beauteous flower when next we meet.
Good night, good night! As sweet repose and rest
Come to thy heart as that within my breast.

ROMEO   O wilt thou leave me so unsatisfied?   125

JULIET   What satisfaction canst thou have tonight?

ROMEO   Th' exchange of thy love's faithful vow for mine.

JULIET   I gave thee mine before thou didst request it –
And yet I would it were to give again.

ROMEO   Would'st thou withdraw it? For what purpose, love?   130

JULIET   But to be frank and give it thee again:
And yet I wish but for the thing I have.
My bounty is as boundless as the sea,
My love as deep. The more I give to thee,
The more I have, for both are infinite.   135

END OF TEST

Notes

Notes

Answers and Mark Scheme

Set A Answers – "Food!" Reading Test Paper

'Real' Cornish Pasties

1   It has cracked down on companies based outside Cornwall producing and selling 'Cornish' pasties. It has given the name 'Cornish pasty' a PGI status.

(1 mark for each different response, up to a maximum of 2 marks)

2   a) It suggests that they wanted to take firm action.   *(1 mark)*

    b) They suggest that the audience is one which accepts informal language, i.e. children/young people.   *(1 mark)*

3   a)

Topic	Paragraph Number
Rules about pasty ingredients	4
What PGI stands for	2
A reaction from a top chef	7
An introduction to the article	1

    1 correct paragraph   *(0 marks)*
    2 or 3 correct paragraphs   *(1 mark)*
    4 correct paragraphs   *(2 marks)*

    b) It has these different kinds of paragraphs because:
    the writer is trying to entertain as well as inform
    it shows a variety of ways of convincing the reader of the truth of the story

(1 mark for either explanation)

4   Simple points made about the article, with limited awareness of how the writer tries to appeal to young people.   *(1 mark)*

Two examples of how the article is trying to appeal to young people, with some comment on how the text has this effect. Some awareness of effect is evident. Two of the three bullet points are addressed briefly.   *(2 marks)*

Shows some understanding of how facts and dates are used to make the article appeal to young people and an awareness of how the language and content affect the reader. Some references to the text are included to support ideas. The third bullet point is only briefly addressed.   *(3 marks)*

Some exploration of how the text tries to affect the reader through all three bullet points. A consistent attempt to comment on all three bullet points. References are used appropriately to support all ideas.   *(4 marks)*

A focused response which explores in detail, with close precise reference to the text, picking out individual words and phrases, how the article affects the reader. All three bullet points are addressed and a high level of awareness is shown by an understanding of different techniques that the writer has used.   *(5 marks)*

Oliver Twist

5 a) "suffered" or "tortures" (NOT "slow starvation" – the question says one word)   *(1 mark)*

b) "suffered" – makes the reader think that they were in pain/had to put up with discomfort
"tortures" – makes the reader think that their pain was terrible/really bad/inflicted by someone else/on purpose

(1 mark for each valid response, linked to the answer to 5a)

6 It suggests that he is greedy.   *(1 mark)*

7 a) Features of Oliver Twist's character from this extract:
  * He is brave (he accepts the challenge to ask for more/he accepts his beating)
  * He is persistent (he asks for more twice)
  * He doesn't care about his fate because he's so hungry
  * He is surprised by his own bravery

(1 mark for identifying any of the above)

b) Features of the master's character:
  * He is not used to being questioned or contradicted
  * He is easily angered
  * He is violent in nature

(1 mark for identifying any of the above)

8 a) It begins with long paragraphs and ends with shorter ones because:
  * The writer switches from narrative description to dialogue
  * The writer builds up the tension by describing the background first

(1 mark for either explanation)

b) It makes you feel sorry for Oliver because:
  * It is the second time he has had to ask
  * He is being well-mannered and reasonable and you would not expect anyone to refuse him

(1 mark for either explanation)

9 The writer wants us to feel sorry for Oliver.   TRUE
The writer is trying to criticise the way that boys like Oliver were treated by authority. TRUE
The writer is trying to give a factual historical account.   FALSE
The writer is trying to entertain the reader.   TRUE

1 correct   *(0 marks)*
2 – 3 correct   *(1 mark)*
4 correct   *(2 marks)*

Why is water good for you?

10   i   It includes facts, e.g. "Water is vital for ensuring that our bodies function correctly"
(1 mark – both reason and quotation needed)

ii   It gives reasons, e.g. " ... <u>because</u> water is responsible for transporting nutrients around the body"/"<u>because</u> ... most of the chemical reactions within our cells take place in water"
(1 mark – reason and either valid quotation needed, but quotation must include the word "because" up to a maximum of 2 marks)

11

Word/Phrase	Effect on the reader	How it creates this effect on the reader
We also lose water by evaporation	makes the reader think that drinking water is important	because it suggests that we need to replace this water
To stay healthy	makes the reader think that drinking water is important	because it suggests that you will be ill if you don't drink it
We should drink at least 6 to 8 cups or glasses	makes the reader think that drinking water is important	because it suggests that there is a great need for it

(1 mark for a quotation accompanied by an appropriate explanation, up to a maximum of 2 marks)

12   a) It acts as a diuretic.
You lose more water than normal.
It makes you need more water than normal.   *(1 mark for any of these responses)*

b) Brackets are used to <u>provide examples</u> of drinks that include caffeine.   *(1 mark)*

13   Simple points made about language or content, with limited awareness of how the writer tries to influence the reader.   *(1 mark)*

Two examples of how the language or content is making the article sound serious, with some comment on how the words influence the reader. Some awareness of effect is evident. Two of the three bullet points are addressed briefly.   *(2 marks)*

Shows some understanding of how the language and content make the article influence the reader. Some references to the text are included to support ideas. The third bullet point is only briefly addressed.   *(3 marks)*

Some exploration of how the language and content in the text try to influence the reader through all three bullet points. A consistent attempt to comment on all three bullet points. References are used appropriately to support all ideas.   *(4 marks)*

A focused response which explores in detail, with close precise reference to the text, picking out individual words and phrases, how the article affects the reader. All three bullet points are addressed and a high level of awareness is shown by an understanding of different techniques that the writer has used.   *(5 marks)*

Set B Answers – "Monsters" Reading Test Paper

Bigfoot of North America

1 • hairy
  • ape-like
  • biped
  • 7 – 9 feet tall
  • 600 – 900 pounds
  • 14" by 8" footprint size
  • 4 toes   *(1 mark for any of the above, up to a maximum of 2 marks)*

2 a) It suggests that:
   • It might not be true
   • There might have been earlier sightings that we don't know of
                                          (1 mark for either of these responses)

   b) It suggests that:
   • They're unusual
   • They're not of a human or recognisable creature   *(1 mark for either of these responses)*

3 a)

Topic	Paragraph Number
A description of a captured Sasquatch	3
An introduction to what Bigfoot is	1
An explanation of what the captured Sasquatch might have been	4
The first sightings of a Sasquatch	2

   1 correct paragraph   *(0 marks)*
   2 or 3 correct paragraphs   *(1 mark)*
   4 correct paragraphs   *(2 marks)*

   b) To make the passage more convincing
       To show that the Bigfoot has been sighted by a variety of people
                                          (1 mark for either of these responses)

4 Simple points made about how Bigfoot is a fake, with limited awareness of how the writer makes
   the reader feel this.   *(1 mark)*

   Two examples of how the article makes Bigfoot out to be a fake, with some comment on how the
   text has this effect. Some awareness of effect is evident. Two of the three bullet points are
   addressed briefly.   *(2 marks)*

   Shows some understanding of how historical examples are used to make the account believable
   and an awareness of how the descriptions of Bigfoot affect the reader. Some references to the
   text are included to support ideas. The third bullet point is only briefly addressed.   *(3 marks)*

   Some exploration of how the text tries to affect the reader through all three bullet points. A
   consistent attempt to comment on all three bullet points. References are used appropriately to
   support all ideas.   *(4 marks)*

A focused response which explores in detail, with close precise reference to the text, picking out individual words and phrases, how the article affects the reader. All three bullet points are addressed and a high level of awareness is shown by an understanding of different techniques that the writer has used. *(5 marks)*

Dracula

5 a) "for I did not know what to do" *(1 mark)*

   b) Because s/he has to read on to find out what the narrator does. *(1 mark)*

6 It suggests that:
   * They disapprove of the narrator
   * They don't like him *(1 mark for either appropriate response)*

7 a) "The old man motioned me in … with a courtly gesture" *(1 mark)*

   b) Either of these quotations, or a summary of them, is acceptable:
   * The man is unusually strong/"grasped mine with a strength which made me wince"
   * The man does not seem alive or human/"more like the hand of a dead than a living man" *(1 mark for an acceptable answer)*

8 a) One mark for a difference that refers to both pairs of paragraphs – commenting on either paragraphs one and two or three and four alone gets no marks. The bit in brackets is not needed to get the mark – it is just to help you understand the answer.

   Valid comments about paragraphs one and two:
   * The writer uses lots of personal thoughts (to show us what he is thinking)
   * The writer uses a lot of self-questioning (to show he is confused)

   Valid comments about paragraphs three and four:
   * The writer describes the old man from the narrator's viewpoint (so that we see him through his eyes)
   * The writer describes the old man from the outside (so that we don't know what he's thinking, to make him more mysterious) *(1 mark)*

   b) It makes the story interesting because it:
   * Creates a sense of mystery
   * Makes us want to read on to find out who he is *(1 mark for either valid comment)*

9 The writer wants us to feel that the narrator is confident.   *FALSE*
   The writer's aim is to entertain and interest the reader.   *TRUE*
   The writer wants us to like the old man.   *FALSE*
   The writer's aim is to build up tension in the reader.   *TRUE*

   1 correct *(0 marks)*
   2 – 3 correct *(1 mark)*
   4 correct *(2 marks)*

The Loch Ness Monster

10 "The Loch Ness Monster is <u>supposedly</u> living in Scotland's Loch Ness"

"this <u>unidentified</u> animal"

"a <u>strange</u> aquatic creature"

(1 mark for identifying two of the above, up to a maximum of 2 marks for explanations of why these examples create a feeling of mystery – see the question)

11

Word/Phrase	Effect on the reader	How it creates this effect on the reader
convinced	makes the reader think that there might be some truth in the monster stories	because it suggests that the men had no doubts/believed what they saw
received several letters	makes the reader think that there might be some truth in the monster stories	because it suggests that the account made other people confess their experiences/come out with stories
claiming also to have seen	makes the reader think that there might be some truth in the monster stories	because it suggests that the account was backed up by other witnesses/other people had seen it

(1 mark for a quotation accompanied by an appropriate explanation, up to a maximum of 2 marks)

12 a) The writer uses the word "thorough" because:
- It suggests that the scientists had done their job properly
- It suggests that the entire loch has been surveyed   *(1 mark for either response)*

b) It is in inverted commas because the writer is casting doubt on whether the monster deserves to be called a monster/whether it really is a monster.   *(1 mark for either response)*

13 Simple points made about language or content, with limited awareness of how the writer tries to make it sound serious.   *(1 mark)*

Two examples of how the language or content makes the article sound serious, with some comment on how the words affect the reader. Some awareness of effect is evident. Two of the three bullet points are addressed briefly.   *(2 marks)*

Shows some understanding of how the language and content make the article sound serious. Some references to the text are included to support ideas. The third bullet point is only briefly addressed.   *(3 marks)*

Some exploration of how the language and content in the text try to affect the reader through all three bullet points. A consistent attempt to comment on all three bullet points. References are used appropriately to support all ideas.   *(4 marks)*

A focused response which explores in detail, with close precise reference to the text, picking out individual words and phrases, how the article affects the reader. All three bullet points are addressed and a high level of awareness is shown by an understanding of different techniques that the writer has used.   *(5 marks)*

Set C Answers – "Down South" Reading Test Paper

Jean Lafitte

1   He established his own kingdom of Barataria.
He claimed to command more than 1000 men/provided them as troops for the Battle of New Orleans.
He engaged in the slave trade after it was banned.   *(1 mark for each up to a maximum of 2)*

2   a) He had a varied life/it contained a mixture of exciting/good/bad incidents.
(1 mark for an answer containing either of these explanations)

    b) His life has been exaggerated/his life is legendary
(1 mark for an answer containing either of these explanations)

3   a)

Topic	Paragraph Number
The end of Jean Lafitte's life	6
Two places that exist today, connected to Jean Lafitte	7
A summary of Jean Lafitte's main achievements	1
The history of a diary about Jean Lafitte	3
A place named after Jean Lafitte	8
Reasons why Jean Lafitte became famous	4

1 correct paragraph   *(0 marks)*
2 or 3 correct paragraphs   *(1 mark)*
4 correct paragraphs   *(2 marks)*

    b) Because it's writing to inform/it's from a reference book/encyclopaedia.
(1 mark for an answer containing either of these explanations)

4   Simple points made about Jean Lafitte, with limited awareness of how the article tries to give the reader a fair view.   *(1 mark)*

Two examples of how the article gives the reader a fair view, with some comment on how the text has this effect. Some awareness of effect is evident. Two of the three bullet points are addressed briefly.   *(2 marks)*

Shows some understanding of how facts and dates are used to make the account believable and an awareness of how the descriptions of Jean Lafitte and his life affect the reader. Some references to the text are included to support ideas. The third bullet point is only briefly addressed.   *(3 marks)*

Some exploration of how the text tries to affect the reader through all three bullet points.
A consistent attempt to comment on all three bullet points. References are used appropriately to support all ideas.   *(4 marks)*

A focused response which explores in detail, with close precise reference to the text, picking out individual words and phrases, how the article affects the reader. All three bullet points are addressed and a high level of awareness is shown by an understanding of different techniques that the writer has used.   *(5 marks)*

Arriving In New Orleans

5 a) coasted   *(1 mark)*

   b) That the roar is either:
      • hideous
      • frightening
      • suggesting that something is being killed or badly hurt
                           (1 mark for any of these acceptable responses)

6 They were eager to see their destination.   *(1 mark)*

7 It is smelly/"odour of mud"/"fetid stink of cesspools"/"smell of burning sugar".
  It is crowded/"teeming streets"/"noisy, thronged streets".
  It is derelict/"only charred timbers among rampant fireweed".
  The people are unfriendly/"The man did not answer, spat to his right".
              (1 mark for any two of the above up to a maximum of 2 marks. Quotations or
                                   explanations are acceptable for a mark)

8 a) Getting off the boat.   *(1 mark)*

   b) There is an emphasis on bad things, e.g. the cow bogged in the mud, the smell.
     There are hints of fear – the "quivering ship", the "gruesome roar", the "red moon crawled".
          (1 mark for including one of the above reasons in the answer. No mark for an explanation
                               not backed up with an example or quotation)

New Orleans

9 The writer wants us to be aware that New Orleans is a smelly place   TRUE
  The writer wants the reader to feel like the accordion maker   TRUE
  The aim of the writer is to scare the reader   FALSE
  The aim of the writer is to put people off visiting New Orleans   FALSE

  1 correct   *(0 marks)*
  2 – 3 correct   *(1 mark)*
  4 correct   *(2 marks)*

10 "seduces" – makes it sound like the place is chatting you up/enticing you/drawing you in like
   a lover.
   "sultry southern heat" – makes it sound sexy or steamy/alliteration "sultry southern" used
   to create a hot, steamy effect.
   "Caribbean colour" – it makes it seem lively and exotic/alliteration "Caribbean colour" used
   to create a lively effect.
   (1 mark for each explanation supported by a quotation from this list of acceptable responses up to
                                       a maximum of 2 marks)

11

Word/Phrase	Effect on the reader	How it creates this effect on the reader
Enshrouding us in dreams	makes the reader think that New Orleans is exciting	because it suggests that it is a place of mystery/fantasy
sweet-tasting cocktails	makes the reader think that New Orleans is exciting	because it suggests that you can enjoy drinks that are better tasting than in other places
laissez les bons temps rouler	makes the reader think that New Orleans is exciting	because it suggests that it is a party town where people are just out to enjoy themselves
laced with voodoo potions	makes the reader think that New Orleans has a darker side	because it suggests that evil and black magic might affect you there without your knowledge
a well-earned reputation for excess and debauchery	makes the reader think that New Orleans has a darker side	because it suggests that people get out of control
The City That Care Forgot	makes the reader think that New Orleans has a darker side	because it suggests that the place is run down and abused

(1 mark for a quotation accompanied by an appropriate explanation, up to a maximum of 2 marks)

12 a) Because a checkerboard has a mix of black and white squares, just as New Orleans has a mix of contrasting neighbourhoods.   *(1 mark)*

b) Because it's an explanation of the French word that comes before it.   *(1 mark)*

13 Simple points made about language, with limited awareness of how the article tries to make it sound an exciting place.   *(1 mark)*

Two examples of how the language makes the article exciting, with some comment on how the words affect the reader. Some awareness of effect is evident. Two of the three bullet points are addressed briefly.   *(2 marks)*

Shows some understanding of how the language makes New Orleans sound lively and mysterious. Some references to the text are included to support ideas. The third bullet point is only briefly addressed.   *(3 marks)*

Some exploration of how the language in the text tries to affect the reader through all three bullet points. A consistent attempt to comment on all three bullet points. References are used appropriately to support all ideas.   *(4 marks)*

A focused response which explores in detail, with close precise reference to the text, picking out individual words and phrases, how the article affects the reader. All three bullet points are addressed and a high level of awareness is shown by an understanding of different techniques that the writer has used.   *(5 marks)*

Writing Test Papers

The bands for writing give descriptions of the main features to look out for in your writing. Different bands have different amounts of marks in them.

For bands with three different marks, check the following:

- If your writing fits everything in that band, but shows no evidence of the bands above or below, give yourself the middle mark.

- If your writing fits everything in that band, but shows one piece of evidence of lower bands, give yourself the lower mark in the band.

- If your writing fits everything in that band, but shows one piece of evidence of higher bands, give yourself the higher mark in the band.

For bands with two marks, you need to do two of the things in the band to get the lower mark and everything in the band to get the higher mark.

For bands with one mark, you need to do everything in that band to get that mark.

It is important to look at the different marks you are getting in order to build up an accurate picture of the strengths and weaknesses of your writing – for example, you might get high marks on composition and effect, but your spelling may be letting you down. If you know this, then you should focus on these areas in order to improve your writing.

Long Writing Task Papers – Mark Scheme

Section A: Sentence structure and punctuation

Band A1
Sentences and phrases are mostly linked with joining words like "and", "but" and "when".
Sentences are simple and may contain lots of repeated words and phrases.
Full stops, capital letters and exclamation marks are used to punctuate sentences, mostly accurately.

(0 marks)

Band A2
Sentences are varied, and more complex joining words like "who" and "which" are used.
Words like "if" and "because" are used to help give reasons and for emphasising ideas.
Commas are used quite accurately within sentences.

(1 or 2 marks)

Band A3
Simple and more complex sentences are used – long sentences and short sentences are used successfully.
Suggestions are given, by using words like "can" or "would".
A variety of punctuation is used with accuracy.
Different types of sentences, e.g. commands, questions or exclamations, are used in order to create more interesting effects.

(3 or 4 marks)

Band A4
The writer begins sentences more skillfully, with words like "usually", "hopefully" etc. or by being impersonal, e.g. "Some people believe that ...".
A range of punctuation is used and this is sometimes done for deliberate effect, e.g. brackets are used to put in asides and thoughts.

(5 or 6 marks)

Band A5

Sentences are varied, depending on the effect that the writer wishes to create.
Simple sentences might be used, but to create effects, e.g. shock or surprise.
Punctuation is used skillfully in order to make the reader speed up and slow down and to make the meaning of the writing perfectly clear.
(7 marks)

Band A6

A wide range of sentence types is used with skill, accuracy and thought to control the writing.
There might be some non-standard sentences, but used for deliberate effect.
There is a very wide range of different types of punctuation used, in order to create a number of different effects.
(8 marks)

Section B: Text structure and organisation

This section focuses on how overall meaning and effect is put across through the way that the writing is organised and planned.

Band B1

Ideas are mainly linked because they happen to be on the same topic.
Points might be put in a list, but not necessarily in any sort of order of importance.
Paragraphs might be used to show some of the obvious different topics in the writing. *(0 marks)*

Band B2

Paragraphs usually start with the main topic in the first sentence.
Paragraphs contain examples.
The writing has some brief opening and closing comments, but they will be fairly brief and undeveloped.
(1 or 2 marks)

Band B3

Paragraphs are written in a logical order.
The introduction and conclusion are clear.
Paragraphs of different lengths are used, e.g. short paragraphs might take the form of a persuasive question.
(3 or 4 marks)

Band B4

Detailed content is well handled within and between paragraphs.
Some phrases like "On the other hand" or "In addition to this" etc. are used to link the paragraphs.
The introduction and conclusion are developed and help to make it more persuasive.
(5 or 6 marks)

Band B5

Paragraphs are varied in length to suit the different ideas being discussed.
Paragraphs are linked with a variety of words and phrases.
Paragraphs are ordered in such a way that the writer might have used them to highlight contrasts, or to be ironic.
(7 marks)

Band B6

The whole piece of writing is organised, shaped and controlled to achieve a range of effects, or to get the reader thinking in a certain way.
Within paragraphs, the writer has used a wide range of links that are precisely and carefully chosen.
(8 marks)

Section C: Composition and effect

This section focuses on the overall impact of the writing and the effect it has on the reader.

Band C1

The writing shows some awareness of the reader.

There is some relevant content.   *(0 marks)*

Band C2

The writing is generally lively and attempts to interest the reader.

The content of the writing shows that the writer recognises its purpose.

Some reasons are given for the ideas and opinions, but perhaps not that many.   *(1, 2 or 3 marks)*

Band C3

The writing is detailed and gives clear reasons for the opinions and viewpoints expressed.

The writing engages the reader's interest.

The writing gives a range of relevant ideas and the writer's viewpoint is clear.   *(4, 5 or 6 marks)*

Band C4

The piece is well written because it uses a range of techniques such as repetition, humour and a consideration of the reader's needs in order to persuade.

The writer's view is consistent.   *(7, 8 or 9 marks)*

Band C5

The tone and content of the writing are appropriate and well judged.

The writing deliberately interacts with the reader.

Content is relevant throughout and is used to support the ideas.   *(10, 11 or 12 marks)*

Band C6

The writing has been done skillfully and the writer is totally in control of the writing type.

The viewpoint of the writer has been maintained throughout.

There is a strong individual style, created by a range of methods.   *(13 or 14 marks)*

Short Writing Task Papers – Mark Scheme

Section D: Sentence structure, punctuation and paragraph organisation

This section focuses on how you choose to organise your writing and how this contributes to its overall effect.

Band D1
Sentences are fairly simple.
Sentences are linked by simple joining words like "and" or "then".
Full stops and capital letters are used with accuracy.
Paragraphs are used to separate the more obvious different topics given in the task.   *(0 marks)*

Band D2
Sentences are varied and use linking words like "who" or "which".
The writing is written in the same tense throughout.
Words like "he", "she", "it", "they" and other pronouns are generally used correctly.
Paragraphs are mainly put into a logical order, as is the detail within them.   *(1 or 2 marks)*

Band D3
A variety of longer sentences is used. This includes those sentences that have been built up from joining simpler ones together to make longer ones and sentences where the word order has been successfully re-arranged for effect.
Words like "completely", "partly" and others which help to make meaning more precise, are used.
Words like "he", "she", "it", "they" and other pronouns are used correctly.
Tenses are used correctly.
Paragraphs are used for appropriate reasons and are put into a logical order.
The detail in them is put into a logical order.   *(3 or 4 marks)*

Band D4
Sentences are written in a variety of ways to achieve interesting effects that suit the purpose of the writing.
A range of punctuation is used – sometimes to create effects.
Paragraphs are of different lengths and the information in them is organised cleverly to suit what is being written about.   *(5 marks)*

Band D5
There is a wide range of sentence structures that use a sophisticated range of verbs and tenses.
Within paragraphs, the writer has used a wide range of links that are precisely and carefully chosen.
There is a very wide range of punctuation used, in order to make meaning clear and create a range of effects.   *(6 marks)*

Section E: Composition and effect

This section is to do with the overall impact of your writing and how well it fits the audience you are writing for.

Band E1
The writing shows some awareness of the reader.
Simple techniques, like repetition, are used.
Content is relevant to the question, but might well be unevenly used. *(0 marks)*

Band E2
The writing tries to interest the reader.
Some techniques, e.g. use of adjectives, are used to help writing, but they might not be very imaginative. *(1, 2 or 3 marks)*

Band E3
The writer interests the reader.
The writer is clearly aware of what type of writing he/she is doing and for whom.
The tone of the writing is consistent throughout. *(4, 5 or 6 marks)*

Band E4
The writing is well written and convincing throughout.
The writer really engages the reader's interest.
There is a very good range of well-chosen details.
The viewpoint of the writer is consistent throughout. *(7, 8 or 9 marks)*

Band E5
The writing has been done skillfully and the writer is totally in control of the writing type.
The viewpoint of the writer has been maintained throughout.
There is a strong individual style, created by a range of methods. *(10 marks)*

Section F: Spelling

This section focuses on accuracy in spelling. Choose the section that best fits the writing.

Band F1
Simple words and those with more than one or two syllables are generally accurate. *(1 mark)*

Band F2
More complicated words that fit to regular patterns and rules are generally accurate. *(2 marks)*

Band F3
Most spelling, including irregular words, is accurate. *(3 marks)*

Band F4
Virtually all spelling, including complex words that don't fit to regular rules or patterns, is correct.
(4 marks)

Shakespeare Test Papers – Mark Scheme

Much Ado About Nothing mark scheme

The mark bands apply to all three Much Ado About Nothing questions.

Find the band that best fits your answer and for every bullet point in that band that you achieve, give yourself one mark within that band, e.g. if you think you are in Band 4 and you have done two of the bullet points, then you should give yourself 11.

Band 1
A few simple facts and opinions about these extracts.
There may be some misunderstandings.
Parts of the extracts are retold or copied and answers may be only partly relevant.   *(1, 2 or 3 marks)*

Band 2
Contains a little explanation, showing some awareness of the needs of the question.
Comments are relevant but are mostly about the plot.
Some broad references to how the characters speak or act.   *(4, 5 or 6 marks)*

Band 3
Some general understanding of the question, although some points might not be developed.
Some comments on the language that the characters use or the effect of the plot on the audience.
Some points backed up with reference to the text.   *(7, 8 or 9 marks)*

Band 4
Some discussion of how the extracts relate to the question, even though all the ideas might not be of equal quality.
Awareness of the characters' use of language and its effects.
Most points backed up with references to the text.   *(10, 11 or 12 marks)*

Band 5
Clear focus on how the extracts relate to the question.
Good consistent comments on the characters' language and its effect on the audience.
Well-chosen quotations linked together to present an overall argument.   *(13, 14 or 15 marks)*

Band 6
Every quotation is analysed in depth with relation to the question and there is an evaluation.
Every quotation is commented on in terms of the language that the characters use, or the difference between what they don't know and the audience does.
Individual words are picked out of quotations and linked into the overall argument. *(16, 17 or 18 marks)*

Useful quotations for Much Ado About Nothing Set A

Act 4 Scene 1

Come, bid me do anything for thee.

    This shows the degree to which Benedick has changed since the start of the play, in that he is no longer a stubborn bachelor.

We'll be friends first.

    The fact that Benedick says this to Beatrice, shows that he doesn't want his newly admitted relationship with her spoiled.

*Is he not approved in the height a villain that hath
slandered, scorned, dishonoured my kinswoman?*

    Here we see the strength of feeling that has arisen in Beatrice and her passionate nature.

o that I were a man for his sake

    The repetition of this sentiment by Beatrice in the scene shows how she feels trapped by society in not being able to take revenge for Hero.

Act 5 Scene 4

*BEATRICE
Do not you love me?
BENEDICK
Troth, no – no more than reason.*

    Here, the witty exchange shows the good-natured banter that is at the core of Benedick and Beatrice's relationship.

*A miracle! Here's our own hands against our hearts.
Come, I will have thee: but, by this light, I take thee
for pity.*

    Benedick shows that he cannot resist teasing Beatrice.

*I yield
upon great persuasion – and partly to save your life,
for I was told you were in a consumption.*

    Beatrice shows her wit and sarcasm, mirroring that of Benedick, showing how they are well matched.

Useful quotations for Much Ado About Nothing Set B

Act 4 Scene 1

BEATRICE
Yea, and I will weep a while longer.
BENEDICK
I will not desire that.

    In these lines, we see how concern is an important ingredient in showing love.

It were as possible
for me to say I loved nothing so well as you. But believe
me not, and yet I lie not: I confess nothing, nor I deny
nothing. I am sorry for my cousin.

    Beatrice shows the audience that words alone don't show evidence of love.

I will swear by it that you love me; and I will make him
eat it that says I love not you.

    Benedick is talking of his sword here and it shows how people often want or need to show their love through deeds and promises.

Act 5 Scene 4

I'll tell thee what, Prince; a college of
wit-crackers cannot flout me out of my humour.

    Benedick's attitude shows that there is nothing so good as being in love.

for man is a giddy thing, and this is my
conclusion.

    Benedick realises how the effect of being in love is to throw a person emotionally and intellectually out of balance.

Think not on him till to-morrow:

    Benedick's comment shows that being in love leads to an absence of care.

Useful quotations for Much Ado About Nothing Set C

Act 4 Scene 1

*You dare easier be friends with me than fight with mine
enemy.*

    Beatrice shows how relationships involve emotional blackmail and conflicting demands.

*Enough: I am engaged. I will challenge him. I will kiss
your hand, and so I leave you.*

    Benedick's words show how sacrifices need to be made in relationships.

Act 5 Scene 4

Do not you love me?

    Beatrice's words show how people are sometimes insecure in relationships and need reassurance.

*Why, then my cousin Margaret and Ursula
Are much deceived: for they did swear you did.*

    Beatrice's words show how people's relationships are viewed differently by the people in them.

*I would not deny you; but, by this good day, I yield
upon great persuasion - and partly to save your life,
for I was told you were in a consumption.*

    Beatrice's sarcastic humour shows how relationships take different forms – not all people would engage in banter like this.

Peace! I will stop your mouth.

    Benedick shows how someone has to take the lead in a relationship.

Romeo and Juliet mark scheme

The mark bands apply to all three Romeo and Juliet questions.

Find the band that best fits your answer and for every bullet point in that band that you achieve, give yourself one mark within that band. e.g. if you think you are in Band 4 and you have done two of the bullet points, then you should give yourself 11.

Band 1

A few simple facts and opinions about these extracts.
There may be some misunderstandings.
Parts of the extracts are retold or copied and answers may be only partly relevant.   *(1, 2 or 3 marks)*

Band 2

Contains a little explanation, showing some awareness of the needs of the question.
Comments are relevant but are mostly about the plot.
Some broad references to how the characters speak.   *(4, 5 or 6 marks)*

Band 3

Some general understanding of the question, although some points might not be developed.
Some comments on the language that the characters use.
Some points backed up with reference to the text.   *(7, 8 or 9 marks)*

Band 4

Some discussion of how the extracts relate to the question, even though all the ideas might not be of equal quality.
Awareness of the characters' use of language and its effects.
Most points backed up with references to the text.   *(10, 11 or 12 marks)*

Band 5

Clear focus on how the extracts relate to the question.
Good consistent comments on the characters' language and its effect on the audience.
Well-chosen quotations linked together to present an overall argument.   *(13, 14 or 15 marks)*

Band 6

Every quotation is analysed in depth with relation to the question and there is an evaluation.
Every quotation is commented on in terms of the language that the characters use.
Individual words are picked out of quotations and linked into the overall argument.   *(16, 17 or 18 marks)*

Useful quotations for Romeo and Juliet Set A

Act 1 Scene 1

Out of her favour where I am in love.
> Romeo is depressed about his love for Rosaline being unrequited.

O brawling love, O loving hate,
O anything of nothing first create!
O heavy lightness, serious vanity,
Misshapen chaos of well-seeming forms!
> The use of oxymorons shows how Romeo is confused.

Love is a smoke made with the fume of sighs:
> Romeo is acting out what he thinks a lover should do, but he has, as yet, no experience himself.

In sadness, cousin, I do love a woman.
> Romeo shows he still has a sense of humour, when with people he likes, like his cousin, Benvolio.

She will not stay the siege of loving terms,
Nor bide th' encounter of assailing eyes,
> Romeo is frustrated that Rosaline does not love him in return.

Farewell. Thou canst not teach me to forget.
> Romeo is stubborn.

Act 2 Scene 2

Her eye discourses. I will answer it.
– I am too bold.
> Romeo is anxious not to mess things up with Juliet.

O that I were a glove upon that hand,
That I might touch that cheek!
> Romeo displays the typically obsessive and exaggerated behaviour of a lover.

O speak again, bright angel! – For thou art
As glorious to this night, being o'er my head,
As is a wingèd messenger of heaven
> Romeo uses the clichéd language of love because he knows no better.

Call me but love, and I'll be new-baptized.
Henceforth, I never will be Romeo.
> Romeo makes strong promises, showing his innocence and strength of feeling.

Useful quotations for Romeo and Juliet Set B

Act 1 Scene 1

So early walking did I see your son.
Towards him I made, but he was ware of me,
And stole into the covert of the wood.
> This shows the secretive behaviour of lovers.

Many a morning hath he there been seen,
With tears augmenting the fresh morning's dew,
> Romeo is acting like a typical courtly lover of the time by showing his emotions to "prove" he is in love.

And makes himself an artificial night.
Black and portentous must this humour prove,
> Romeo's behaviour is stereotypical of a depressed lover.

Could we but learn from whence his sorrows grow,
We would as willingly give cure as know.
> This shows how others get concerned when someone is supposedly in love.

ROMEO
Dost thou not laugh?
BENVOLIO
No, coz, I rather weep.
> This shows how lovers get things out of proportion and lose their sense of emotional balance.

Act 2 Scene 2

What man art thou, that thus bescreened in night
So stumblest on my counsel?
> This shows how a lover's behaviour can seem shocking and unsettling.

JULIET
Art thou Romeo, and a Montague?
ROMEO
Neither, fair maid, if either thee dislike.
> This shows how lovers make extreme promises that they can't necessarily keep.

For stony limits cannot hold love out –
> This shows how love gives a person strength.

Alack, there lies more peril in thine eye
Than twenty of their swords.
> This shows how love makes a person reckless.

Useful quotations for Romeo and Juliet Set C

Act 1 Scene 1

O where is Romeo? Saw you him today?
Right glad I am he was not at this fray.
    This shows how Romeo's mother is concerned for his physical well-being.

Could we but learn from whence his sorrows grow,
We would as willingly give cure as know.
    This shows that Romeo's parents are concerned about his emotional well-being.

BENVOLIO
It was. What sadness lengthens Romeo's hours?
ROMEO
Not having that which, having, makes them short.
BENVOLIO
In love?
ROMEO
Out –
BENVOLIO
Of love?
ROMEO
Out of her favour where I am in love.
    These short, sensitive questions show Benvolio's concern for his cousin.

Act 2 Scene 2

What man art thou, that thus bescreened in night
So stumblest on my counsel?
    This shows how Juliet is, at first, shocked by Romeo's behaviour – until she realises who it is.

I would not for the world they saw thee here.
    This shows how quickly Juliet reveals the strength of her feelings for Romeo.

But farewell compliment!
Dost thou love me? I know thou wilt say 'Ay' –
And I will take thy word. Yet if thou swear'st
Thou mayst prove false. At lovers' perjuries
They say Jove laughs.
    Juliet shows here that she thinks that she is rushing into a relationship with Romeo, but can't stop herself.

O swear not by the moon, th' inconstant moon,
That monthly changes in her circled orb,
Lest that thy love prove likewise variable.
    Juliet is worried that Romeo will prove to be fickle in his feelings.

My bounty is as boundless as the sea,
My love as deep. The more I give to thee,
The more I have, for both are infinite.
    Juliet shows how quickly she has completely fallen for Romeo.

Notes

Notes